Before I Let You Go

Stories for My Grown Son

Kirsten Wreggitt

For Cody Wreggitt

Cover designed by JD&J Design LLC

ISBN 978-1-7751321-1-0

INTRODUCTION

I was petrified we would have a girl. Everything about having a girl was horrible to me—the princess parties, the fear for her safety, and the emotional roller coaster ride. But mostly I was afraid she would be like me: suicidal, unable to make brave choices, and trapped inside a body she didn't love. I was terrified I would have to face that mirror in two places every day. When Cody came, I was pretty sure we wouldn't try again. We had a boy and who knew what the gods might have planned for a second baby.

Cody was an only child, for better and for worse. It was all snails and puppy dog tails and now he is 22. He has grown up and somewhere in there, I did too. I am now watching him prepare to leave home, and I'm thinking about all the things I would like to tell him. I feel a terrible urgency as our daily time together is coming to a close. I want to share all the things I've learned about life up to now, but there is just never a good time.

I want to tell my son who I really am, beyond being his mother. I want to save him some mistakes and sorrows. I want to help him relate to himself and to women in a different way. I want him to find more peace and love in his life, sooner than I did. And I know that other moms (and dads) want these things for their kids too.

The face-to-face conversations are too real. There is uneasiness with that level of vulnerability, and none of us is dying. Don't you let the dying say what they want to say? So instead our conversations revolve around schedules and work and leisure. Nothing deep, nothing real. But the words are too hard to hold in. They bubble up at the back of my throat and pulse just under my skin. I searched for an outlet and found that I could share my stories on paper and ease the pressure inside.

I wrote Cody these stories about my biggest life lessons: stories of love and sorrow, and stories of triumph and failure. I let my simple average life spill out onto paper and searched for the grains of truth I could share with him. These stories are more than stories to only Cody.

They are stories to you, other mothers: you are not alone, as we have walked similar journeys.

They are stories to you, millennials, the next generation: you will have a hard time understanding the generation that came before you, just as I have struggled with understanding the generation that came before me.

They are stories to you, teenage girls: you will also find yourself in dark places. Know that you, too, can rise.

They are stories to you, men: you who are curious about what life looks like through the female lens.

They are stories to you, all the shifters and changers: you take the situations you find yourself in and work to make the most of them.

And they are stories to myself: I write in forgiveness, compassion, and loving kindness, as I didn't know the mistakes I would make or the successes that would come from my efforts.

I hope as you read these stories that you will see yourself reflected in them and know that our life journeys are not that different. Though our circumstances and experiences vary, we are all on the same journey. We are journeying to know ourselves and love all of it, the good and the messy. This book may spark you to want to share your own life lessons with others, and I encourage you to do so. When you finish with this book, please pass it on to someone else in your life who might benefit from my perspective.

Here's to the lessons written through our lives and to the stories written from our hearts.

Dear Cody,

I know we don't talk about the really serious stuff. It is too hard. I brushed off my parents' attempts at wisdom too. Who I am to tell you what I have learned in my life? Besides, "the world is so different now," you'll say.

Yet there is an urgency to connect with you, as you will be moving on soon, out into the world. The opportunities I'll have to share these thoughts with you might never happen. So I am going to put them all into this book, and maybe you will read it, pull it out when it is appropriate, or reflect on it when I am gone. In here, I can say the things that catch in my throat. I can say the things that make your eyes roll. In here, I can safely share what I have always wanted to tell you but the time was just never right.

As I gathered the stories I put in here, I realized there will always be something left to say. I cannot anticipate all the situations you will find yourself in. I cannot pre-think about what lessons I have learned that you will appreciate. I just looked back and shared the biggest things that came to mind. And in looking back, I noticed something: this book may not have been just for you.

This book has also been for me, maybe even more than it was for you. Through writing it, I had to wrestle with my life and come to grips with it. I had to relive some painful times and find enough peace to get it down on the page. And I had to acknowledge that maybe my lessons will not be your lessons, and so I cannot prepare you fully for this world.

Be strong out there, my son. Look for the love and kindness in others. Forgive yourself when you make mistakes, and enjoy the journey.

When things get hard, and they will, I take comfort in the way you came into the world. When you were being born, as your shoulders crested, you stuck your fist out above your head. It was your Superman proclamation to the world. "Here I come! I raise my fist in defiance—whatever the world throws my way, I am strong and I am ready." And now I can let you go with love.

Here are the things I couldn't tell you.

Love,

Mom

SECTION 1: BE WELL

Postdating Contentment

Cody, age 22. Me, age 44.

I can't believe you are now 22. I let my parenting years slip through my fingers, like every other part of my life. When I was 13 or 14, I can remember wishing I was 16 and able to drive. When I was 16, I remember wishing I was 19 and able to drink. When I was 19, I remember wishing I was finished university and able to get a job. When I was 23, I remember wishing I was a mother. When I was a new mother, I remember wishing you would sleep through the night, and then walk, and then talk, and so on. I have lived my life waiting for that next thing. I wished it all away, and I feel like I missed it. From now on I will try desperately not to look ahead, for fear that if my gaze is there, I will miss something here.

What if I hadn't wished it all away? Would I remember better what a new baby smelled like? Would I remember better the joy of academia and being on the precipice of adult life? Would I have made better choices as a parent and been fully attentive to you? I can't go back, no matter how much I want to. Instead I can only learn from these mistakes and try to remain in my body, not my head, as my days continue.

"When I …" is the most dangerous opening of a sentence. It is postdating contentment and happiness to some future date and basing it on some expected result or outcome. When I get married, when I have a child, when I graduate from university, when I get this next promotion, then my life will be … happy.

I'm not sure I am cured from this even now that I recognize it and its danger. There are plenty of days that I imagine some "When I's" and how my life will be better then. The biggest one right now is "When I retire." A close second is "When I am fit."

I was beyond fit in 2010. That year was the pinnacle of personal trainers, dedication at the gym, and crazy clean eating. I was very close to having abs you could count. I was a single-digit size and people commented regularly on how I looked. All my life I had strived for this. I can remember looking at my thighs as a young teenage girl and wishing they were smaller, and here I was at 39 still striving. For some reason, in 2010 it all came together. Maybe I was able to starve myself the longest that year. I looked fantastic.

I was waiting for some crowd to cheer, for the doorbell to ring and some fanfare to be waiting outside, but nothing happened. In fact, my weight and fitness had nothing to do with how content I felt. I still felt an equal amount of discontentment. The discontentment had shifted to my work, it shifted to my stretch marks (you can't really get rid of those), and it shifted to finances. It was as though there were an allotted amount of discontentment with my life, and no matter what I fixed, I was able to find other things that still needed fixing.

I tried gratitude, meditation, yoga, a new job, another new job, walking, writing, and any other possible distraction you can think of. I tried friendships, charity, community, and connection. Nothing worked. The burden of the "When I …" was a leech on my soul, and if I managed to save a part of me from it, it simply found another host. I couldn't kill it. I wish I could tell you I've figured out how to maim it permanently, but I haven't.

I didn't know the perils of "When I …" at the beginning of my adult life. Everything was a "When I …" back then. The major life milestones were still to happen, and so I couldn't know how wide and deep my discontentment was until I had crossed some of them off the list. After I graduated, got married, had a child, got a great job, I could measure my discontentment. It was just as big and wide. I am still spending my lifetime trying to shrink.

I am a planner and a dreamer. I set goals. I imagine and visualize the outcome of my efforts. I have calendars with due dates and monthly rituals of measuring progress. I live for the future I am creating. But I've realized something while dragging my discontentment with me. I might live for the future and the achievement of the "When I …," but I can't really live in any other time than now. My discontentment motivates me to plan change, but I cannot let that steal from the current moment.

Each of my life's major milestones was checked off with a brief glimmer of joy. Happy wedding photos, first birthdays and first steps, raises and promotions. I let those joyful moments slip through my fingers so fast, and I was quickly strapping on my hiking boots for the next mountain to climb. But there was always another sea of discontentment to paddle across. I wish I had rested longer in those joyful moments. I kept postdating my contentment to some future time, even though contentment was right there around me.

Being Okay with the Size I Am

Cody, age 20. Me, age 43.

My doctor asks me, "Do you know how much weight you've gained since your last physical?"

"No. I don't own a scale. And I don't really want to know," I sheepishly reply. I want to tell him to stuff it. Of course I know I am bigger. I've had to buy new clothes as I busted out of my former size!

I get into my car and drive home. I have to change for work and I catch a glimpse of myself in the full-length mirror. I stand there and look at myself.

"So gross. So jiggly," I think.

I step into the closet to find something to wear. I pull on a skirt and top and then stop in front of the mirror again. "Nope. Not that skirt. Look at your bumps." I change my skirt.

Dressed now, I go to the kitchen to pack my lunch. There is leftover spaghetti, but I tell myself I shouldn't eat the carbs. I could buy my lunch, but there aren't any healthy choices nearby. I certainly don't want to eat fast food and feel people judging me when I do.

I finally head out the door and feel my thighs rubbing together and listen to my nylons making a *swish swish* sound with every step. I get into the car and start driving. It's only after this long morning of berating myself that it finally hits me.

"What if I am okay with being the size I am?"

This question puzzles me. It feels like I have just heard that the world is round, not flat. It is a paradigm-shifting thought. I grapple with the enormity of it. If I simply decide I am okay with how I look, my

11

internal dialogue will change forever. What will I say to myself? Will there just be silence? Could there be room for something new? I have heard the same loop for over 30 years–talk about an earworm! What if there are only crickets to replace my chatter? What will I do?

The next morning I feel inspired to empty my closet of all the clothes that don't fit me right now. I can't believe I haven't done this before. Heck, I was once a professional organizer. I look at the sorted closet and I feel lighter. All the reminders of my size change are bagged up to go. I didn't realize the subconscious burden that clothes had on me. Every time I got dressed, I had to sift through that pile and remind myself that I no longer fit in those clothes. Even if I didn't consciously think about that, I subconsciously knew how few of them fit. I think about all the restrictions I have put on my life up until now. All of the conforming, attempting, and hiding can end. Gosh darn it, I can now put on a swimsuit and go swimming. The diatribe of self-hatred can cease and I can just live. Instead, my day can be about showing up with love, with wisdom, and with grace instead of thinking, "Despite my size … ummm … please notice that I … ummm …".

I want to be healthy, but I can make healthy choices for health reasons, not to fit into a single-digit size. I can make healthy choices out of love for myself instead of hate. I love the power in that.

How many times have I given up on some experience (or at least ruined it by overthinking my appearance) because of my self-consciousness? Sunbathing, going to the gym, doing yoga, and attending fancy formal events. I know you saw me sitting on the sidelines and couldn't understand why.

I am not my body. My body is a tool to carry around the most important parts of me: my heart, my mind, and my spirit.

I will stop wriggling into the too-tight jeans and berating my thighs and belly bump. Instead I will put on clothes that let me move and let me breathe so I can concentrate on living. I don't care what the number is on the tag. I will cut it out if it helps. Instead I will ask, "Do my clothes allow me to show up?"

I want to run because I want to, move because it feels right, and eat because I need nourishment. I want to live because I have life, and it is now, not when I'm the perfect size or the perfect number on the scale. I want to end the focus on what I am not, and instead focus on what I am and how I am gifted.

It is funny how life gives you the lessons you need to learn. I have always been heavier, but I got really heavy just before I got pregnant with you. Probably not the best health combination. In fact, I topped out my weight at the peak of my pregnancy at 211 pounds, and I didn't lose much on the day you were born. Having postpartum depression didn't exactly make for ideal conditions to lose the weight either.

As you grew, I could envision you entering school and needing to go places with me and having to introduce me to your friends. I wanted more than anything for you to not be embarrassed of me, and so I tried my best to get into shape. I went from a size 22 to a size 14/16 before you entered school and stayed there during your elementary school years. I was so relieved that you didn't have to be embarrassed of me. I still didn't love my body and it still stood in the way of me doing a lot of fun things. I was still too embarrassed to wear a swimsuit, put on a climbing harness, or jump in the air. But I was average enough.

When you went into high school, I had more time to myself. I was working with Dad and we had pretty good cash flow, so I invested in a few personal trainers. I was able to get my weight down and even get into a size eight now and then. I can remember sitting in the stands at one of your football games. I had long hair and a pair of jeans and a sweatshirt on. You told me that one of your fellow players said your mom was "hot." I was so relieved. It was certainly better to be embarrassed that your mom was hot than have them make fun of your mom for being big, like they did other larger moms. I couldn't fully hang on to that weight and size, but I starved my way through your most important years looking pretty good.

I wanted to be sure that I looked good enough for you. I starved myself, sweated, stressed, and strained just so that you never had to turn away and go, "Yep, that's my mom" while feeling sick inside. And now, things have slipped again, and the hate-filled earworm is taking back over. I am thinking things like, "I might have to do another health push to look good at your wedding," and "I've got to look good for my future grandkids." This battle runs deep. Can I really be okay with the way I look, or will I always strive to fit into the world's expectations?

I tried hard not to speak those expectations out loud, but I did. I know you heard me say I was fat or out of shape or that I was a cow and shouldn't be eating something. I see you working out and trying to eat clean, and I worry that you now hear those things in your head too. Our narrow definition of beauty is pervasive. I want you to be healthy, but I also want you to love yourself. Having both body health and mental health is such a tricky balance. It's one I haven't won yet.

Good News

Cody, age 14. Me, age 37.

I am awake again and its only 2:30 a.m. Everyone is sleeping. The house is dark and I'm in a cold sweat and swirling. I strain to listen to the meaning behind the creaks and groans of the house. Was that someone on the porch? Was that a car in front of our house? Do I hear someone opening the back gate? I can barely hear anything over my heart pounding in my ears and I can't swallow. I imagine the choices I might have to make. Will I yell out for you? Will I reach for my phone to call 911? Will Dad have to watch me die first or will I have to watch him? I need to untangle myself from the damp hot sheets, but I cannot expose myself to any more darkness. When I close my eyes, I see horrific torture at the hands of some intruder, a nightmare while awake.

I let the alarm go off even though I have been staring at the clock for hours. I get up feeling drained. I didn't get enough sleep, and today will be a long workday.

"You are quiet this morning," Dad says.

"I didn't sleep well last night," I mumble. "I kept thinking someone was coming to hurt us. Do you think we could get a security system?"

"Ummm, no," Dad scoffs.

I shrink. He doesn't understand. I can't help how I feel late at night. I can't stop the images and I don't want to feel this way either. I don't try to explain and instead head to work. I double check that the door is locked behind me.

The workday is long and I am thankful to be making my way home. I haven't got much energy after not sleeping well last night, so I head right to my chair and curl up to watch some TV. The news comes on and it's a never-ending stream of violent images. Dad and I sit through it because at this time of night there isn't much else on. He selects the next show. It's a crime investigation series and I can feel my anxiety level rise. What if I didn't sit through this?

"I think I'm going to go upstairs and read," I say.

"Why?" Dad asks.

"I'm just tired of the same storyline. Some woman getting killed by some violent man," I say tiredly.

"Oh," Dad says and raises his eyebrows in realization.

"What if we pick something else?" Dad offers.

"How 'bout just a rom com?" I suggest.

The nightmares begin to lessen over the next few weeks. I have stopped watching the news and I am choosing lighthearted media instead. I am feeling better and I don't feel like I have to cross the street when a man is approaching when I'm walking alone anymore. I have stopped worry about getting on an elevator alone with a man too. I have also stopped planning where to hide. This is an easier way to live.

"Hey Mom, can we go to the movies?" you ask a few weeks later. You point at the latest action movie trailer on the TV.

"That one might be for you and Dad," I say.

"Oh Mom, you are such a softy," you joke.

I am okay with that. There are movies I cannot watch, just as I cannot watch the news. I want to stay informed and I want to be entertained, but my overload threshold is lower than some people's. If I don't monitor how much bad news goes in, the night fears start again. I let you tease me and send you to the movies with Dad. I will stay here alone with no security system and no escape plan. I will watch a chick flick and feel safe and sound. I have created enough security by keeping what is going into my mind more safe. It is a more beautiful world than the one the media causes my imagination to conjure up, and I am happy to have found this sheltered space.

Apathy

Me, looking back.

I was that kid who wanted everyone to belong, everyone to have a friend, and no one to suffer. I used to watch the Jerry Lewis Labor Day Telethon for the Muscular Dystrophy Association and beg my parents to send in as much money as they could. When I thought about my career, I knew that it had to impact the world or people in some way, so I looked at social worker, biomedical engineer, and environmental biologist. I really thought that it was just a matter of time before we saved the world from all that ailed it. I was an idealist and an optimist. I was empathetic and engaged.

And then life happened. I needed a job. We had a family. I climbed a little corporate ladder and soon I was mired in so much obligation that the idea of helping save the world seemed like such a small priority. The world's problems were too big. I had my own problems. Besides, doesn't it seem like nothing we do makes any difference?

I struggled with whether that was true. Are the problems really too big? Are my problems not the world's problems? Can't we find some solutions?

When I turn on the evening news, I don't see any evidence of our problems getting smaller or hear stories of triumph and success. I see more pain and suffering, day after day. Having 24-hour global news doesn't help either. At one time, I would not have had heard about tragedy across the globe. And if I did, I might have only heard a news story once. Now I hear about any given instance of pain and suffering from across the globe three or four times as it crosses my path through different media, reaching me through TV, radio, and Twitter.

On top of the onslaught of bad news, I am hardwired to notice the bad stuff. It is a survival technique for us humans. I remember negative images longer because of the emotional responses they trigger. And I tend to share those same negative stories with others, and they do the same. Bad news travels fast. We are not good at sharing stories of success.

I feel like Sisyphus when I watch the news. I am pushing a rock uphill for eternity with no end in sight. I feel despair, and then, eventually, even I, a soft-hearted empath, feel apathy. What is the point of even trying? Except that I know that people are also hardwired to help. We are meant to create social bonds for survival. We need each other. We need to be helping and to be helped, but even the most concerned among us can be driven to apathy from the never-ending images of suffering.

I've heard it said that "good news isn't news" and that people won't watch it. Maybe. But what good is it if everyone watching the news sits there in apathy and inaction in response to the magnitude of the problems? What if there were more on the news than bad news? What if it truly informed us of the complexity of the world's problems, explored and shared ideas of what people are doing to make a difference, and highlighted some of the successes that we are surely having? News does not present solutions. It does not present hope. It is picking a scab, not helping things heal.

Self(ish) Care

Cody, age 21. Me, age 44.

There are a thousand things on my to-do list today. Send the proposal. Write a blog. Get my social media wrangled. Call a friend. Clean the kitchen. And on and on. Down near the bottom of that list are meditate and exercise. Those are my self-care items, but they seem so selfish. There are so many more important things to do. How can I possibly stop and make time for these?

And so I decide I won't. I know I should, because my joints continue to hurt. My back aches. My tummy is widening. I don't have very much energy. I let my body pay the price today, like most days lately. I try to work but my mind feels cluttered, my heart races, my thoughts swirl, and my productivity drops. I'm paying a bigger price than I care to admit. "But I'm busy!" I tell myself. "I'm doing all the important work! Right?"

It is an enormous hurdle for me to step away from work and take some time for myself. I wonder if I will ever be able to quiet the voice in my head that says, "Keep working." I view taking those one or two hours a day for self-care as selfish. So selfish. "How dare I take time for myself. There are people who need me!" I suffer from such inertia that it is hard to get over it to make self-care happen. But what if I can reframe it?

What if I don't think about myself as engaged in self-care at all? What if I think about exercise and meditation as a service to others?

I try to imagine the benefits my clients would receive from me taking care of myself. Being strong would allow me to have the necessary energy to help them. Being pain free would allow me to focus and to fully serve. Having a clear mind would allow me to be present.

I can step away from my work today with that thinking. I will put my self-ish care to the test and see if it helps me serve.

Choosing Joy

Me, looking back.

Most people mindlessly answer the question "How are you?" at least a few times a day. I used to respond, as the majority of people do, with "I'm fine." And then one day I decided to respond differently. I was working at Sears and not feeling my best. As a manager, I knew that my mood could affect many people, and so when my colleague asked me, "How are you?" I dug deep and said, "Fantastic." I wasn't choosing to respond truthfully, but instead I wanted to respond intentionally. I saw her step back a bit and she said, "Really, why?" I could feel a little door open inside of me. I peered through it for a reason to feel fantastic. I couldn't immediately see one, but that tiny door shone a little extra sunlight on my heart right then. So I said, "Because I can choose to be!" She smiled, and I could see she was thinking about that as she walked away. I could have just said, "Fine," and neither of us would have had that moment of reflection. I actually felt more fantastic just in saying it. This tiny shift in response created a change, not only for me, but often for the person asking.

By choosing to respond with extreme positivity, I actually started to feel that way. The standard response of "I'm fine" did not create resonance, but "I'm fantastic" somehow told my mind that we had something great going on. I would feel more positive and more grateful.

That's not all. Every time I answered that way, the person who asked me usually asked why, and I had to ponder that. I grew a list of reasons why. I focused more on the positives that were in my life, even when things were not so great.

But here is the secret in all that. I didn't just respond that way—I chose to respond that way. We have a choice every single day, despite what is going on in our lives, to choose joy. We can chose to see the positive in every situation, we can choose to share the positive viewpoint, and we can choose to be more than fine. It is not an easy choice.

Joy is hard work! We are hardwired to look for threats and sources of pain, but if we are conscious of this predisposition, we can choose to look past those things. We are conditioned to respond with a safe and nondescript platitude. We don't fully check in on our own feelings and we don't often intentionally try to shift them. I am not saying that you shouldn't acknowledge the feelings you do have, but you can also choose to replace them. You can focus on the tiniest of good things. You can choose joy.

And I suppose I should define joy. For me, joy is the acknowledgement of what is—no matter what "is" is—and being present and standing in awe at the wonderment of life. Even in great pain and suffering, we can be fully present and amazed at the intensity of the feelings we are experiencing. We can be fantastic and fabulous simply because we are aware. This takes energy and effort, but it is worth it.

Responding to "How are you?" with "Fabulous" might seem insincere at first, but for some reason, the more you look for the positive, the more you actually see and feel it. Think about Sunny, our golden retriever—she is a never-ending fountain of positivity. She is happy we wake up. Happy we come home. Happy she has breakfast. Happy someone comes to visit. Her positivity is infectious, and you cannot help but be lifted up by it. We all need to spread more joy. So rock someone's world today, and respond with something more than "I'm fine."

Church

Me, looking back.

I know you aren't one for religion or spirituality or woo woo stuff. I get it. I'm not much of a believer either, but I have been. Or rather, I have been where believers are.

Church has come into and out of my life a few times. As a child, I attended church regularly with my parents. We went to one of four churches on Sunday, not because we were church hopping, but because our parish owned four churches in our area. We rotated where church was each Sunday to warm each building once a month with our singing, knees, and communion. Each of those churches was filled with old woodwork that creaked and groaned. They all had a smell of musty oak, faint incense, and dust that even now I associate with blue-haired ladies, sombre funerals, and long, boring sermons. That smell makes me squirm in my seat.

Each of these churches had redeeming qualities too. Some had beautiful stained glass windows, others had padded kneelers or less stiff pews. It was hard for people to decide which churches should be sold off as the congregation shrank, and the upkeep expenses grew beyond the budget.

I was married in one of these churches, and it was actually the same one my parents were married in. We have the same staged photos on the steps of the church with our wedding parties smiling in innocence. Long before that, I was an altar girl and I served the minister by lighting and snuffing the candles, moving the bible, and other altar girl duties. All I really remember about that was the long minutes of kneeling in my altar girl robes, getting hotter and hotter and trying hard not to faint.

As a teenager, I joined the church's version of talent

development—the Girls' Auxiliary—and we travelled to other small Northern Ontario parishes and competed in dance, singing, choral speaking, and drama. We giggled at dirty magazines at the back of the chartered bus, snuck out from our billet's homes late at night, and pretended we were pious and devout and innocent during the day.

I also attended a church camp retreat of some other Christian denomination that put the fear of God into my teenage soul and resulted in more than one person repenting in tears after the long sessions of brainwashing. I think I "came to Jesus" every year and wondered when I would actually feel His presence in my heart and feel washed anew. Every year, a day or two after going, it was all forgotten.

When I moved away from home, I left the church behind. I was studying science, and there was little room in my evolutionary logic for creation and God. I didn't completely reject things, but my skepticism grew. I did wonder, though, at the hand of God in "chance" mutations and in the intricate beauty of biological systems, and I certainly did not attend church.

Dad and I graduated from university deeply in debt, and I was a bit broken from the self-flagellation necessary to keep my scholarship. I had little self-esteem or energy left to apply to jobs with companies in cities I didn't know. I was already sure they wouldn't want me. So I resigned to follow Dad back to Northern Ontario and begin a life there. The results of that move were no jobs in my field, a new baby, and rock-bottom finances. We persisted, and eventually we clawed our way into a home of our own. This small victory did not fill the brokenness I still had. With postpartum depression and a business that required 60-hour work weeks, I was desperate for a lifeline. One of our employees had a church he went to.

Our employee didn't preach, he didn't cajole, he simply offered that sometime I might join him there. It was a different church than I was used to. Sure, the Jesus was the same, the message was the same, but the smell and decor were different. It was fresher, four or five times the size of my past churches, with young people, not just pew after pew of bleeding lipsticked, pruned, sour-smelling octogenarians.

I can remember going with him one Sunday morning and feeling self-conscious that everyone would know I was new and that they would see the Jesus-sized hole in my heart. And then there was the music. I grew up on the repentant ancient hymns of the Anglican Church. I still wonder why no one has written any new ones. But the songs at this church had live guitar and drums! No sad organ being played by a congregation member. The singing filled all the spaces and wrapped its arms around you and squeezed the tears from your eyes. I am sure our window installer grew tired of me sniffling beside him each week.

I leaned heavily on that church and the members of our little bible study group for young couples. I had God, who would help take care of us. We had trust and faith where we once only had emptiness and dread. Then, slowly, I was able to hold myself up again and I was able to look around me. I started to notice the hypocrisy and politics, the judgment and condemnation, and I had to leave.

I haven't gone back to a church except for weddings and funerals and the other odd event that is held in one. Church was important for me when I was at the bottom. It wasn't the building. It wasn't the music—though that was pretty special. It was the community. I didn't expose you enough to church, and I know you would reject all attempts to go there now. But don't completely discount its purpose. There may be a time in your life when the need for community outweighs your rejection of religion.

I have been able to replace church with my own community for now. A few close friends that can wrap their arms around me. But if friends waver, there are buildings filled with immediate, ready-built community just waiting for me.

I have also found my own religious experiences when I am out in nature. Its music, made of the choir of birds, the lilt of a summer breeze, and the rhythm of waves on a shore, can squeeze the tears from my eyes just as those hymn once did. I am in my own church and washed in the spirit, at least for a few moments.

Hearing the Small Voice

Cody, age 21. Me, age 44.

I just got an Instagram account. Not because I really need another place to share photos and proclaim the brand of me, but because there might be some business value and I wouldn't want to miss out. This is ludicrous, and yet I've gone and done it.

There are so many messages coming my way: how I should look, what to wear, where to vacation, what my house should look like, etc. This noise is so loud that it's hard to ignore. Without even realizing it, it seeps in and I start to take notice. I change my hair to reflect the current trends. I buy the latest gadgets and join the latest social media platforms. I look twice at the newest cars, thinking I might just need the surround sound and parking assist features. Unless I start living under a rock, it's hard to escape these messages. They are on the TV, on the radio, in my social media feeds, on website sidebars, and don't forget in the product and lifestyle articles shared by my favourite content curator.

Don't get me started on the courses, coaches, programs, etc. that I am supposed to need as an entrepreneur. It seems that if I am not automating, optimizing, targeting, and engaging in another new way every few months, I will be left behind. The entrepreneurial noise is deafening to the point that I could be learning some new program every six months and never actually get any work done.

Sure, some of this noise is helpful, but where in there do I listen to my gut about what is working for me and what makes me happy and fulfilled? I need to get grounded at least twice a year, and to do that I need to tap into the quiet voice inside of me that knows what I desire and what will truly make a difference in my life.

Grounded. So many meanings. Both "to be well-balanced" and

"to be prohibited from recreational activities," like a child being punished. In both situations, we are trying to even things out, take away the extra stimulation and emotional charge, and bring things back to a sense of calm order. Just like a child benefits from a little time out to catch their breath and regain their emotions, I too need my grounding time to come back into myself.

I have to unplug. I have to have a few days in a row with no external influences. I have to create space and quiet. Vacations are usually the easiest way to do this. Summer vacation is naturally filled with a complete escape as we travel, leaving our world behind. It is harder to find a time in winter to escape, when Dad and I are so busy. But I have gone on retreat right here in our house. I usually do this near Christmas. I black out my schedule and put an out-of-office message on my phone and email. I precook meals to create the sense of having a caterer. Each of those days, I start the morning slowly, with meditation and yoga. I spend those days in quiet contemplation and end each day with reflection. I turn off all electronics to give myself permission to be unreachable. It has been possible to create space in my life even without running away.

When I do this, I can sift through all the noise and really hear what is true for me. My small voice, the one that has never done me wrong, can be heard, and I listen. Sometimes I have to ask specific questions, like: What is working for you? If you could have the perfect day, what would it look like? If you could amplify one part of your life that brings you joy, what would it be? The answers to the questions from the small voice are the answers I really need, the guidance I really need, and the ideals I truly should aspire to.

The returning to my small voice's wisdom cannot end there. For just as surely as I write down what my small voice has to say, I will return to the noisy environment of my life and quickly get swept up into the cultural ideals of our time. I need to refer back to my notes regularly and keep my goals and ideas in front of me, or the media will paint over and rewrite them as fast as it can.

My small voice doesn't suggest amassing the latest gadgets, pursuing wealth, or burying myself in status symbols. Instead, my small voice encourages me to slow down, create connection with loved ones, and enjoy more of the simple things in life, like a good meal, a walk under the stars, and a good book. It always knows what's best. I just can't always hear it.

SECTION 2: UPON REFLECTION

Plan Less

Cody, age 11. Me, age 34.

"How will we know what to see along the way? What if we can't find a place to stay?" I say, trying to keep the panic out of my voice.

"We will be fine," Dad reassures me. "There is always a Walmart parking lot or a hotel," he adds.

We are planning a road trip to Oregon, then down the coast to the top of California, and Dad doesn't want to book anything. Three weeks of vacation with nothing planned or booked. I am freaking out. I know how we got here and it's my fault, but I'm still uncomfortable with this.

I am a planner—I even do it for a living. But when I plan, I set up an expectation of that plan in my head. I fill it in with vivid images. Vacations are not excluded from my planning and its resulting pre-lived predictions. I try to control the fun down to the tiniest detail. I imagine the fun times at a waterpark, what each campground will look like, the cozy campfires we will light, and I let the expectations get cemented in place. In the weeks leading up to a vacation, I have time to picture it all. So much so that when we finally go on vacation, I am constantly comparing my vision of what I thought would happen to what actually happens. It is never as idyllic as my fantasy. Dad wants to end my disappointment. He wants this trip to be different, so he asked me to not plan anything.

I agree to try it his way on this big road trip. No campsites planned, no itinerary set, no research done in advance of things to see and do. I don't feel sure of this, but I am willing to give it a try, because disappointment due to my expectations is no fun either. I don't notice much as we are driving along the road the first day. I am too busy trying to anticipate where we will sleep. I scour the maps. I flip through the campground guides. I watch road signs for campsite icons. Then I switch to imagining campground after campground turning us away because they are full and then us sleeping on the side of the road only to be awoken by the police. Of course, we find a site that night at the first place we try. And it is a beautiful place.

Today, I try to breathe a little deeper. I vow to wait until after lunch to start planning where we will stay. We still find a lovely site. I begin to feel different on day three. Today my stomach relaxes. I wait until around 2:00 p.m. to look for a place, and we find a beautiful spot to stop for the night. It turns out that it gets easier. My white-knuckle grip has loosened as I stop trying to control the fun and instead let the fun find us. By the time we reach the top of California, I am feeling a little better about this. We have stopped for sand dune boarding, river rafting, and spontaneous extra nights at the best campgrounds.

I am still nervous, though, when we pull into the well-advertised tourist spot in the old-growth forest. Plastic oversized figurines. Loud speaker voices. Pomp. Circumstance. And a pretty hefty admission price. You are oblivious to the garish nature of this place and are just so excited that we have stopped because you are ready to stretch your legs. I stand in the shade of the van and hide from the signage, gift shop, and carnival feeling of this tourist stop. It is a blight in the midst of the towering peaceful forest. It feels wrong. It feels obscene. I close my eyes against the glare. When I open them, I look away and instead look at the forest across the road. There, hidden in the shrubs, I notice a campground sign. It's small and homemade, and I could have easily missed it. The campground looks to be down a quiet, grassy road. It feels so welcoming and such a contrast from where I am now. Without even going into the gift shop or welcome kiosk of the tourist stop, we get back into the van and drive across the road.

The front porch of the main house is the campground office. It is quiet and unassuming. The owner comes through the door from the house into the office and greets us.

"Where are you from?" she asks.

"Canada," I answer.

"Well, welcome! What can I help you with?" she inquires.

"We need a campsite for tonight and then in the morning we will probably head over to see some old trees, I guess," Dad responds.

She raises an eyebrow as Dad says, "I guess."

"I get the feeling you don't want to go there?" she probes.

"Well, not really," Dad says with a sigh. "We had hoped for some old trees, but we certainly don't need an amusement park to enjoy them."

She reaches under the counter and hushes her voice. "Well, I might just have something that will fit the bill." She pulls a paper from behind the counter and turns it so Dad and I can see it. It is a photocopied hand-drawn map. It has mileage markers and trail landmarks to help navigate. She is sharing an uncommercialized version of the forest, the version I was hoping for.

The next morning we set out on our own self-guided tour using her photocopy as a treasure map. The first stop is a hike deep into the forest. The trees are magnificent, but what is even more amazing are the fern-covered cliffs rising on either side of us. We are in a creek bed with mossy covered rocks at our feet and we are surrounded by these cliff faces full of lush ferns. It feels like we are in some fairy tale land. You agree and call it "Fern Gully." It is magical. The world falls away, and I can't hear anything except the sounds of the forest. We get back in the van and drive a little further. This stop is a hike to see an ancient twisted tree. The redwood is a few hundred yards off the highway and looks as though someone grabbed the top of it and twisted it to wring it dry.

We stop a few more times for grandfather trees that dwarf us at their base. Stretching our arms around the trunk, all three of us together, we cannot make it even a quarter of the way around. Dad looks like a miniature version of himself when I take his picture and you look like a wood sprite. It is quiet and glorious and I am so grateful to the campground lady for her gift of this version of the old-growth forest.

If I had planned this vacation, we would have probably booked the most advertised places and done the tourist-infested sites. Instead we are on the road less travelled with no place to be but where we are. Leaving ourselves open to adventure, the locals often share the secret places beyond the advertised sights. I love this vacation now. I love not planning the fun. I am not anticipating the next stop—I am here paying attention, and loving what I see.

On Being an Opening

Cody, age 21. Me, age 44.

I don't have all the answers. I wish I did. You have just asked me, "What is the point of all this?" and I don't have a satisfactory response. I was better at answering the questions you asked when you were younger, like "Why is the sky blue" and "Where do babies come from?" But here we are gazing into the existential abyss together and I am wrestling with my own rationalizations. They are too hard to share with you, except maybe here.

I have spent so much of my own life reflecting on what I am doing here. I struggle with it. I worry that maybe I will never find it, and then how would I reconcile that? Is it any wonder that we have a world filled with depression, war, greed, and idealism? But I have persisted with this question, and the closest thing I've found to finding peace is aligning myself with a project that is greater than my own life. Then my life will have purpose, and that seems to have taken the sting out of living and dying.

I met a spiritual teacher a few years ago. I don't think that was her official profession, but that's what she felt like to me. She asked me why I was here. What was my purpose? Together, we spent a few good hours exploring those questions, and we landed on: "I am an opening, I hold space for others to see possibility in their lives." Pretty woo woo. Do you see why I can't talk to you about this? Let me try to explain.

I am an opening; a place of newness, a threshold to pass over, a crisp breeze. When I am in conversation with someone, we gaze across at each other and we bring together our energies and invite something new to be born. The safety of this connection allows for possibility and the honesty allows for creativity. Where there was once heaviness, now there is light. Where there were once obstacles, now there are possibilities. Where there was once hopelessness, now there is renewal. It is my role to ensure the space is safe and to provide honest support. I aim to provide someone with a reflection of themselves, a clarity of their power, or a crucible in which to fire their ideas. I am an opening for people to experience a moment of abundance to carry them forward.

That is enough for me. To feel like I showed up for someone else, to provide them with a moment of hope. But I know you are still struggling with your own existential crisis. I've been there; do not fret. Go deep inside yourself and there you will find a never-ending source of light and love that will overcome the darkness.

How do you find it when sometimes it seems so faint? I know you will, because I have stood looking over the edge into the well of loneliness and been unable to see the light at the bottom. I just jumped and hoped. I crawled and wriggled my way. I spread my eyes wide open in the pitch darkness trying to see when there was nothing to see, and yet somehow emerged on the other side. I know darkness so thick that I am afraid to breathe for fear that I will suck it in and fill my lungs and suffocate. It is a darkness where my arms ache, where my mind spins the tale again and again that life is not worth living, that there is no purpose, and that no one will miss me when I am gone. Why not get it over with now? But then … there will be something that holds me here. The thought that maybe tomorrow will be better, the sight of a child, or the sunrise. And all these things are hope. They are glimmers that guide me along in this long tunnel of darkness to the end of my life.

And what if I still never really know why I am here? I still must eat. I still must drink. I still must sleep. And I must love. And love? Even if that is all there is, that changes everything.

Miscast Roles

Cody, age 10. Me, age 33.

I am sitting in the parking lot at work, crying. I don't want to go in. I don't want to face another day in there.

I hate my hair. It is spiked and fierce and a little too severe. It is my "bitch" hair. It is a representation of my role on stage and part of the costume I wear.

I hate my suit. It is stiff and fierce and a little too severe. It is my "power" suit. It is a representation of my role on stage and part of the costume I wear.

I hate my face. It is drawn and pointed and a little too severe. It is my "confident" face. It is a representation of my role on stage and part of the costume I wear.

Every morning I get up to go to work here, I have to step into the dressing room to get stage ready. My character is a successful business manager, the leader of a team, and the messenger of the latest corporate direction. I have been in this role for a long time. There have been many acts, and I must stay in character for hours and hours. Luckily I am well-rehearsed and most days manage to maintain my facade. They don't know. They don't see behind my costume; at least I tell myself they don't.

I think my staff hate me. I'm about to go into a staff meeting I planned. We are going to dig into unresolved issues and see what I can do to improve. But first, here I am, sitting in my car crying. Yep, there is nothing left. The mask is washing off. I cannot get into character, but I don't like my role anyway. I've been miscast. I have to dig deep and stretch every day to identify with this character, and I feel I often come

41

up short. There will be no standing ovation for my ability to act all these years, and it has taken me seven seasons before I have finally seen that. It is time for me to step off the stage to look for my next gig.

I wear a mask here as a protection against the regular conflict. It isn't conflict with others. The conflict I am really avoiding is within myself. I am living outside of my values and doing things I don't want to admit to. I am selling out on my staff, upholding my role as messenger, but I don't want to be so cold and unfeeling. I want to include my staff as people, people with families and aspirations. I want to include the future of the planet in our decisions about distribution and vendors. I want customers to examine their consumerism and question their purchases as wants or needs. This is the kind of nurturing that I cannot bring to my job here. I have power, but not love. I need to work where I can have love. This is no longer the character for me, and I will take a final bow and let the costume fall away.

The Lie of Having It All

Cody, age 8. Me, age 31.

I am getting you ready for your concert at school. You are finishing grade three. I have missed so many concerts already. All I can do to contribute to this day is tuck in your shirt and help you pass your belt through the back loops. I can help you find your dress shoes and add a clip-on tie. I can only dress you and wish you well. You look smashing for your concert, and I imagine how it will go. I will ask you about it tomorrow and you will answer with little detail, some version of "It was fine." I will have to enjoy my own imagined concert instead. I won't get to see this one. I remember my own concerts so well and how much I loved seeing my parents watching me. They were the only ones I was performing for. You won't have me out in the sea of faces.

I work tonight as I have worked many other nights and weekends, causing me to miss parent-teacher interviews, track and field days, and other school milestones.

I want you to know I was not always this absent. I know you can't remember the first two years of your life, but I was there for that. Really there. Dad worked while I cared for you, and then our lives shifted and my work changed. I made a choice to work in a career that has me missing these milestones. I wish it could be different.

It is a lie to say we can have it all as women (and men, too). There is only a finite amount of time. The lie our culture sells us is that we can care for our families, have an amazing marriage, work in a high-powered career, volunteer in our communities, and still have time for ourselves. The reality is that something gets sacrificed in the process. I am trying to give you a better life with more stability and security, but it is taking me away from you. I may miss the best years of your childhood. I may miss you running into my arms when I come to pick you up. I may miss your concerts at school. I may miss the bruised knees with band-aid kisses. Forgive my choices. I cannot be two places at once, but I am seeing you on that stage today in my head and you are brilliant. I am not in the sea of faces, but I am proud of you just the same.

Mortality—The Ultimate Worst-Case Scenario

Cody, age 13. Me, age 36.

I am lying inside a white tube. My head is cushioned by flannel cloths but pinned to a bed inside a caged mask. I have ear protection on, but it seems inadequate when I can feel the sounds from the machine throughout my whole body. It is like lying on railroad tracks waiting for the train to come. I try to breathe like I am meditating. I am not claustrophobic, but this contraption can bring it on. This is my second MRI in just a couple of weeks, and they are looking at my head and neck to see why I have had a headache for over a month.

At first I just wanted the pain to stop. I wasn't overly concerned that I had a headache—I have had headaches many times before. But at the two-week mark, I knew this was different somehow. There were no outward signs of my suffering until my eyelid began to droop. That wasn't normal. That really changed things. That made it real. I wanted the pain to end, but I also began to think about the bigger questions in life: Have I had a good life? What is left on my bucket list? Am I afraid to die?

You are only 13, and I think about what I will miss. I will miss you finding true love, knowing you as an adult, and perhaps watching you raise a family. I think about writing down what I would want to share with you about those major milestones in life. I think about my own life and what milestones I might have left.

There isn't really anything urgent left on my bucket list that I need to experience. It is hard to believe. Somehow all those dreams and things we imagine for our lives don't seem as colourful and critical when we get down to the truly important things. We have travelled a bit, and along the way I learned that people are people, they just live in a different climate and cultural and economic circumstances. I have achieved sufficient personal success and also realized that it wasn't the secret to happiness anyway. I have found love and had a child. So really, not much left undone.

The only tough question remaining is whether I am afraid to die or not. Many people take consolation in some version of heaven when they are dying. Believing that this is not all there is allows them peace in their life ending. I don't believe in heaven per se, but I do believe in something. Maybe just the passage of my energy back into the collective, but right now I am having to really examine this. I need to get comfortable with the finality of this life.

I think about death in terms of two other experiences: fainting and falling asleep. Not many of us go to bed at night petrified of falling asleep. We lose conscious thought, have no experiences we can really remember, and seem to be okay with the nothingness. I think that if we can do that every day, we can embrace our own death.

I have also fainted. I was feeling very ill while camping with Dad. I was standing talking to him in excruciating pain and simply fell backward in a faint. What was interesting was what happened while I was unconscious. It was glorious. I felt warm and safe. I was standing in a field filled with birds singing and flowers in full bloom. It was colourful, peaceful, and pain free. That experience has left me with the peace that the human body has some wonderful mechanisms for pain management and that going deep into oneself is a lovely place.

This test is to see if they can find the source of my headache. A month after it came, it went. I might never know why it came. This is the closest I have come to a near-death experience and the wrestling of all the big questions that go with that.

I don't feel that much different, but there is definitely a line drawn in my life now: before my headache and after. I am coming to grips with my mortality, and if I am no longer afraid of that, then I have conquered the ultimate worst-case scenario. Everything else should be a cinch.

Grow Your Grit

Cody, age 15. Me, age 38.

The sky is starting to lighten this morning. It is still amazing to me that the day dawns. How incredible it is that the thick blackness can fade from black to light blue in such a short time. The sun; I don't always notice it's rising and setting. The more I think about that, the more I feel so disconnected. We are not meant to be bustling around doing business and creating products and chasing information. We are meant to be more connected to the earth and let it nurture us. We are meant to be aligned with her rhythms and seasons.

I need to share this with you, give you a taste of being immersed in nature, and I have to do it soon. You are turning 15 this summer. Soon you will have part-time jobs with your own schedule and your own commitments. I decide this is the summer to make this lasting memory with you while I still can. Grandpa isn't exactly young either; he turns 62 this summer. I have always wanted to go on a canoe trip with him. I think it's time.

Committing to going on a five-day canoe trip with Grandpa, you, and Dad makes me nervous. I have to pull my weight equally because there are two canoes and so much gear. I have to paddle as much as anyone to navigate the whitewater rapids, carry as many packs, prepare as many meals, and set up as many campsites. I am determined to be an adequate member of our team.

We select an outfitter in Northern Ontario to help with the gear. We can't bring everything with us from Calgary, and this will make it easier for my parents too.

The outfitter suggests a relatively easy five-day canoe trip with class 2 rapids. There is no need to hurt ourselves, since everyone except

Grandpa is a whitewater beginner. Grandpa and I split the cost of a brand-new Kevlar canoe, which he will haul up north to the Missinaibi River for the trip.

The outfitter meets us at the train station. We are going to ride the train up to a stop in the middle of the bush and jump out with all of our gear. She has another canoe, paddles, life jackets, and food for us. We have each packed our clothes and sleeping gear into our own packs to carry. I decide against bringing too many things, since I know I will have to bear the burden of every ounce of stuff. I choose my clothes carefully and decide to give what I wear a workout.

"Here is your food barrel. It's heavy now, but it will get lighter as you eat things. Don't worry that the cheese is not refrigerated. It does fine without refrigeration. It just gets a little greasy but tastes so good when you are tired on day three. Eat the steaks tonight and don't forget to tie your barrel into a tree each night, as there have been lots of bear sightings this year," the outfitter explains.

The hairs on the back of my neck go up and my heart beats a little faster. I am terrified of bears. I try not to let the look of panic cross my face. I want to be a brave participant, not a burden.

"There is some bear spray packed, hopefully you won't have to use it. I know you asked for a beacon, but we have so many trips out right now that I don't have one left. So unfortunately you won't be able to signal for help. I don't think you guys will have any trouble though. We will be picking you up in five days at the bridge. If you are not there at the end of day six we will send someone in to find you. So don't get hurt on day one, or you will have a long wait for help!" she finished, laughing at her joke.

The train arrives and we load everything on, canoes and all. Grandpa tells the ticket collector that we want off at the head of the river and he nods. Tourists pile on and everyone settles into their seats for the ride. We decide to get some food in the dining car, since it will be the last meal someone will cook for us in a real kitchen for five days.

A few hours later we feel the train coming to a stop, and the ticket collector stops by our seats and reminds us that this is where we get out. I look out the window. It is complete wilderness. The tourist passengers begin twittering with each other wondering whether there is something wrong with the train. They don't consider that this could possibly be a planned stop. Before I can reconsider, we hurry to jump out and catch the canoes filled with our packs as the train staff slide them out into the shrubs and brambles at the side of the tracks. We are here, wherever "here" is. The tourists stare in disbelief that someone would willingly get out here.

"There is only one way home now. Down river!" Grandpa says enthusiastically, and we all chuckle. It takes us a few minutes to get ourselves sorted and out on the river. We are not practiced at loading and unloading ourselves yet, but I'm sure over the next few days we will master that. The beginning of the river is a lovely paddle through a grassy swamp. The river is pretty wide here and it is easy going. We aren't quite an hour into our canoe trip when another canoe with an older couple in it slides up beside us.

"Nice day for a paddle," the man says.

"Sure is," Dad replies.

"We hear it is shallow this year," the man shares. Just as quickly as they came, they are a few canoe lengths ahead of us and then out of sight. We lumber along with our wide-based canoes and heavy packs. We are not seasoned canoeists, but we are up for the challenge.

Grassy turn after grassy turn we paddle, looking for the marked campsite. An hour after we expected to be there, I finally see the tent sign high up in a tree and we pull over to set up camp. It is already almost dark. Dad makes dinner and Grandpa, you, and I set up the tents wearing our headlamps. After dinner we tie the food barrel in a tree, and get into our tents. I can hardly sleep. The tents are on a sloped riverbank and I feel like I have to keep crawling up or I will slide feet first into the river. I also can't stop thinking about bears. Before I know it, Grandpa is rattling the tent ready to start the day.

Today there should be some white water! I can hear the burbling sounds a few turns in the river away from the first set of rapids. We pull the canoes over to the side and Grandpa has us walk along the rapids mapping our route. We look for "tongues" of water that will give our canoe enough volume to float, but in so many places there just doesn't seem to be enough water. It has been too dry. We get in the canoes anyway and start down the rapids.

"Hard left," Grandpa shouts at me as I side stroke to make the canoe weave through the rocks.

"Thatta girl," he adds, as we make it into the tiny space between boulders where there is enough water. My paddle clunks against the rocks under the canoe and I can see the bottom coming up fast ahead.

"Gotta stop here," I shout and stand up. I jam my foot and paddle into the boulders beside us to slow the canoe. We each grab a towline and walk in the white water.

The water swirls around my knees making it impossible to see the bottom. I feel my way through the river rocks and bump my ankles on boulders I can't see in the watery swirl. I snag my sandal as it gets wedged between two rocks. It is slow going and the water pushes us along even though it is fairly shallow. The canoe pulls and bumps over the boulders. I am plunged up to my hips in water without warning as I step into a deeper passage. I worry about getting hurt. Our pace is sluggish and we are miles from help. We can't afford any injuries. Half an hour later we are paddling again. That should have been a five-minute fun run through the rapids and instead we are already trying to make up time.

At the next set of rapids, Grandpa and I begin the walk to map out the path again. It doesn't look good either.

"We have the rental canoe. I say we run it," Dad says to you. Grandpa and I decide to baby our brand-new canoe by walking it

50

through the rapids as quickly as we can and wait at the end to see you shoot them. You and Dad are all paddles and smiles. Grandpa takes pictures of the passage—arms flailing, wide grins, and whoop-filled joy. Now that's what this trip was supposed to be filled with!

Our slow pace takes most of the relaxation time out of the day. We don't have time to fish or swim, but Dad and you break into song to lighten up the mood and we all laugh. I decide to throw a fishing line into the river as we paddle along. I probably won't catch anything as we are moving so fast, but I want to pretend we might catch one. The next two days are pretty much the same: we find ourselves still paddling or slogging along a portage or up to our knees in the river when we should be swimming or fishing.

On the third night, we come around a bend in the river, and crossing the water in front of us is a big black bear. My heart leaps into my throat. It is nowhere to be seen on the shore beside us as we pull up to the spot where it crossed. But I can smell its hot skunky musk and see its wet paw prints on the rocks. This is my greatest fear, and I would have been more than happy to have completed this trip without seeing a bear. Not five minutes later I spot the tent sign in the trees.

There are not many places to pitch a tent in this overgrown bush. The designated campsites are nice because they have a clearing for tents, a fire pit, and usually a log or two to sit on. We are going to stay here because there is nowhere else to stay. Bear or not. I get busy making dinner and try not to think about it. The goosebumps form without warning when any twig snaps off in the bush though.

The evening light is fading. I swallow my pride and turn to Grandpa.

"Do you know where the bear spray is?" I ask.

"I'll dig it out of the pack. Why? Are you going to sleep with it?" he teases.

"Yes. That bear is too close for comfort and I won't sleep

51

otherwise," I admit sheepishly.

I crawl into my sleeping bag and clutch the bear spray in a death grip under my pillow. My skin is damp and I am listening so hard to the bush sounds that my head starts pounding. I don't think I am going to sleep tonight. Luckily the long days of paddling have worn me out and a restless sleep finally comes over me. The morning light arrives uneventful and so welcome, and I uncurl my fingers from the bear spray to start the day.

Our food barrel is getting light. It is a welcome change, but it doesn't shorten our portages. We still have two canoes, paddles, fishing gear, and eight or so packs to carry. You and I carry paddles, life jackets, fishing gear, and two packs each, one on the front, one on the back, on the first trip of each portage. Dad and Grandpa carry canoes. On the second trip, everyone carries a pack and someone carries the food barrel. Every portage is two trips and the heat and mosquitos are relentless.

Today's portage is two kilometres and we have to do that twice. Our campsite is at the end of it. On the first trip I vow not to look around the campsite. I am so tired. I just pretend we are still portaging and turn around and head back to the start for the second load. When we arrive the second time, I notice that the river is a wide gravel bed down a little cliff from our campsite. The water is very shallow, only about a foot deep. I know my swimsuit is in my pack but I can't be bothered to look for it. I am sweaty and stinky and my clothes are ripe after three days of canoeing. Without a word to anyone, I strip to my bra and panties. What is different about that and a bikini anyway? I run down the sandy cliff and lay down in the river. The gravel has formed little bathtub shaped shallows and I relax down into one and let the water run over me. Soon you, Dad, and Grandpa are all lying in the river in your underwear too. It is good to be alive. We all sleep so well.

Today is our final day and I can hear thunder in the distance. The wind whips up and whistles through the pine trees. It is undeniable that a storm is coming, and we unpack our raingear and keep it handy at our feet in the canoes. The air takes on an uncharacteristic coolness after the heat of the past few days. We set out on the river and wonder how long we have before the rain comes.

There is nothing left to look forward to today except getting somewhere that has a hot shower, but we have a lot of miles before then. An hour into our paddling the rain starts. I grab my raincoat and put it on. The rain soaks my hands and runs into my sleeves. I don't have rain pants but neither does anyone else. It was one of the things we decided against in an effort to pack light. The rain comes harder. It begins falling so hard that we are yelling to each other over the sound of it on the river. The water dripping off the brim of my hat is a steady stream and my pants are now soaked.

"Can it rain any harder?" Dad shouts up at the clouds, taunting Mother Nature. She responds with some thunder and the deluge continues. The wind starts buffeting us too. It is straight into our faces. We are paddling downstream, but with this headwind it seems like we are not making any gains. I watch the shore beside me with each stroke. It looks like we are only moving a few inches ahead each time. I dig in and pull harder. Despite all my effort, I feel the wind through my wet clothes. My teeth start to chatter and I ask to pull over to the side and put my polar fleece on under my rain jacket. That takes the chill off and we paddle on for a few hours until we finally arrive at the bridge for our pick up. The rain lessens to a drizzle as an arrival present.

Grandpa starts unpacking the canoes with us, but he seems slow and confused. He slurs something to me and stumbles up the embankment. I follow him with a load and grab his hand. It is ice cold and his fingernails are blue. So are his lips. His teeth are chattering and he can't really tell me how he feels. You and Dad continue with hauling the gear up to the side of the road.

"Dad, get some dry clothes on right now," I command. "I think you have hypothermia." We are all drenched from the waist down, but the rest of us seem warm enough.

"Okay," he says and tries to open his pack. His fingers won't work on the clasps, so I step in and unlatch them. There is nowhere to change here on the side of the road but there doesn't seem to be anyone around either. It takes Grandpa a while to get his pants, underwear, and socks off. He finally pulls on some dry underwear over his sticky damp skin just as the outfitter drives up. We all laugh at her timing and we get Grandpa dressed and into the warm truck.

We have a four-hour ride to our vehicles. The truck is loud on the gravel roads and we are all too tired to talk. I am amazed that it is over. We made it through, portages, black flies, bears, and all. And still we smiled and laughed. We all dug deep inside ourselves and found the ability to manage all of the challenges and discomforts and test our own grit.

You can't get that kind of challenge in our suburban life.

I watch the sun set over the trees. When I am deep in nature, there is no one else I can rely on for fortitude; I have to rise to the challenge. This is how to test who I really am. This is how I get up close to nature and see myself in her beauty. This is what I wanted to share with you, and I am so glad I did.

Midlife for Women

Cody, age 18. Me, age 41.

I hate rush hour traffic—the start and stop, bumper-to-bumper pressure cooker that just makes me want to leap from my vehicle and run off into the wilderness. I try to focus on remaining calm. I pop my lavender essential oil diffuser into the lighter socket to fill my car with a calming scent. I tune the radio to a non-news station, and I look around at all the other drivers and try to wish them well on their drive home. There is a well-dressed woman beside me and she is talking to her little passenger. I imagine she just picked up her child from private school and now they are heading home to start making dinner together. There is a teenager and his dad driving on the other side of me. I imagine he is working on getting his driver's license. His dad is probably inwardly hanging on for dear life while outwardly showing support and fearlessness while they drive home together. In front of me I can see a minivan filled with kids and the little TV monitors hanging down into their view. I imagine the mom has packed the kids some snacks and is driving them to dance practice and music lessons. Families in cars doing what families do and I can't stop the tears that start to fall.

Here in rush-hour traffic it hits me: I am all alone in my car. I don't need to drive you anywhere anymore. In fact, you don't need me much anymore at all. My work as a mom is done. The sobs drown out the radio and my tears make seeing the road more difficult. I feel a sense of relief that I have time to myself, but I can't believe it is over. Eighteen years seemed liked it was going to be such a long time, but now that they are over, what am I to do? It has been my job for so long, to love you and nurture you and help you find your independence. And now that you are independent, who am I going to be? This should be a welcome beginning, but I am uneasy with the new-found freedom.

I have started to test my freedom with some business ideas and I am making mistakes. I am having false starts. I am bumping around on my baby-deer legs learning to walk again. I suppose you could say I am having a midlife crisis. That term conjures up purchases of ridiculous fancy cars, out-of-the-blue divorces, changes in careers, and wild wardrobe switches. That's the extreme side, but this is the less visible one, the guilt. I have guilt and I don't know what to do with it. It is the guilt of finally having the time and resources to do what I want after years of putting my needs on the back burner. It feels like I have a candy stash; so indulgent, so selfish. I find myself looking around to see who might steal it from me just as I am about to unwrap and savour the first piece. I also worry that it has it gone stale.

This is where the uneasiness and bambi legs come in. I am so used to my role as Mom that I don't know who I'll be as me. I can't really remember who I am. I think I remember loving art and poetry. I think I remember wanting to save the world and trying to make a difference. But I've put much of that aside, and now I look like a teenager trying on a new identity each week. I'm trying to find myself again. I hear myself saying things like: "That doesn't fit." "That doesn't feel quite right." "This feels good but I'm not good at it yet." I am stumbling around and I think people are judging my short attention span and remedial execution while I try things on.

I wipe my eyes and pull into our driveway. So much sadness and guilt in one car ride. I turn off the car and a shiver of fear goes up my spine. I am halfway through this thing called life. Time is so short. Can I find myself fast enough to do something with the rest of my life? I haven't seen many vibrant women in their second half, and I worry that I too will simply disappear. I wonder if it is the embarrassment of starting life midway that keeps women behind closed doors. I go into the empty house and sit in my chair. I turn on the TV and let the colourful images slow my thoughts. Sitting on the couch watching television is easier than trying to create a new life. But I've seen that future play out. I've caught glimpses of those women on cruise ships and in coffee shops. They have a masked bitterness to them that seeps out through their pursed lips and polite but curt responses. I don't want to be one of those women.

I turn the TV off again and pace the floor. I can't believe how quiet it is and how hard it is to be alone with my thoughts. My chest is so tight and I feel a restlessness that I just can't shake. It is as though a door has slammed and I am standing staring at a woman in the mirror that I haven't seen in decades. I should feel like I've accomplished something, but the accomplishments were yours. I feel like I should have earned something but instead I feel stripped of my titles and purpose. I can't catch my breath. I want to hurry up and find my place, but I can't seem to do much more than pace the room again. I feel like I am searching for something that I cannot find. More than anything, I am afraid that if I sit down I might never stand up again.

Hope and Conviction

Cody, age 18. Me, age 41.

I am here again. That place that feels like there is nothing worth getting out of bed for. I am between jobs and I feel listless and worthless. Even though it was my own decision to leave my job, I feel too tired to reinvent myself again. I know being an employee was not a great fit, but I don't know the first thing about starting a business, which is the most logical next step. I think of all the education I have gained and now I am throwing it all aside. I think about the careers I've left just as they were starting to pay off. This thinking is only making the well I'm digging deeper. I am not sure I have the energy to make another change.

There is something more scary under the surface too. It is a question that grips me when I feel like I am at the bottom. I lie here thinking, "What is the point?" Life is just a pile of work and uncomfortable situations and then you die. Why would I want to put my two feet on the floor let alone shower and get dressed? Inertia and maybe even depression are taking hold. And yet, I swing my legs out of bed and head for the tub.

Part of me wants to wallow in things and just succumb to the feelings that possess me. It isn't easy to be with these hard feelings. There is another part of me though that pushes against that. The smallest, quietest part of me, says, "Come on now, love. Let's get out of bed. Even if things don't get better, you've given it all you've got." What a wise small voice.

I think this is the voice of hope. It isn't as though the voice is saying, "If you get out of bed, things will be better," or "Look for the silver lining." It is simply asking me to get dressed, show up, and get to action. It doesn't promise success or happiness. It doesn't promise results. It just asks for effort. I get out of bed and I start to build my business.

I am telling you this because I am amazed that my voice of hope is present even at the very bottom of my well. It is such a small voice but it is here. I'm not actually sure I can survive waiting for the turnaround, but hope gently nudges me to at least move. It is the harder of the two options. Lying in bed would be easier.

I think hope knows that aside from sleep, rest, and maybe some healing, nothing of value will find me lying in that bed. Opportunity isn't going to come knocking on the door. Maybe a friend or some family might come alongside my bed, but more likely I could go and find that support by rising. Movement is my stake in the ground. Two feet, one in front of the other, is my "fuck you" to the weight of depression and inertia. It might get me down, but it cannot stop me from taking action.

So when you look around at our world and it is colourless and bleak, know that I've been there too. But more importantly, know that I found hope there, and that you might need to look for it, but it will be there for you too. It is hard to recognize at first. It nudges, it is quiet, but it is not meek. It demands action. There, in the worst of times, you could resign yourself, sit in your grief and depression, or you can rise, get into motion, and put one foot in front of the other.

I don't know what motion might look like for you in your future, but it is motion you need to look for in those darker times. I'd argue against those people who say hope is not a strategy, and instead say, if you listen to hope, you will find a strategy. When I am lying in bed pulling the covers up over my head, I don't hear, "I hope everything works out," I hear, "I cannot and will not give up, there is something left here worth striving for." I don't know what it is, but I know I have to rise to find it. I want you to rise too.

SECTION 3: LOVE

We Cannot Run Away from Each Other

Me, looking back.

I often fantasize about running away or leaving my current life. I imagine living in the wilderness away from people and our culture. I want to be a wild woman relying only on me and Mother Nature. This fantasy is usually when I'm bored with how things are going or when I don't want to deal with a tough situation. But mostly when I'm bored. What a privileged thing to even say, but life can be pretty darn boring most of the time. I thrive on change, and when things get a little routine I dream about escaping and becoming someone else.

I got married really young. I was 21. I essentially never knew myself outside of a family, as I went from the household with my parents to the household with Dad. You came along not long after. When I fantasize about running away, I think about escaping alone to be just me. Not because I don't love the two of you, but because I want to know what life would be like outside of other people's needs and concerns. What would it be like to go and do anything you wanted with no one to answer to?

I've read some books about women who went away from their families to be alone for a year. I have friends who take six weeks' vacation without their loved ones. And as delicious as that sounds, I am coming to realize that I cannot run away. Even with these small hiatuses, those women come home to their lives. Life was just on pause. The whole time they were away they were still a player in their worlds. They were just acting from a distance.

No matter how far away I imagine I could go, I would still be who I am. I would still be your mother. I would still be a wife to Dad. I would still be me inside my head no matter where I was physically.

The fantasy seems harmful at first because my heart aches for something else. I wish I could run into the dream and leave this all behind. "Calgon, take me away!" But then the fantasy actually heals me. It reminds me that I cannot really escape from who I am. It is my signal that I'm bored and that I need to shake things up and bring more colour back into our lives. I need that more than Dad, and he humours my thrashing about in our average life.

Slowly, I am also coming to realize that my real work in life is to love what is. I cannot throw it all away and become something else. How can I instead look at my life and love it? I have the privilege of choice and I have an obligation to be grateful.

Puppy Love

Cody, age 15. Me, age 38.

I can hear the clank of dishes and the warming crackle of the kettle as Dad starts our day. I do love my French press coffee. I get myself and Dad a mug and pre-flavour them just how we like it: no sugar for me, but a bit more cream; one and a half teaspoons of sugar for Dad and some cream. He presses the coffee and we sit at the table to sip in our sleepiness and let the warm liquid bathe us awake. Peaches, our golden retriever, is waiting at his feet with her head on his foot. She is aware of his breathing, aware of whether he is merely shifting in his chair or if he is rising to go. She keeps an eye on the tilt of his coffee cup and gauges whether it is empty or not. She observes us with such precision that we end up noticing ourselves.

"Where are you today?" I ask. It is my usual morning question. I want to know if he is working at the shop or in a customer's house.

"I'm in the shop," he says. This means he can work on his own schedule and he will be home for dinner.

Peaches flinches with each of our exchanges, listening for special words or tones. Did I say walk, treat, Peaches, daycare? Her head relaxes onto Dad's foot again when she realizes we didn't include her.

Dad finishes his first cup and sets it on the counter. He will take his second cup to go. He heads to the front door with his familiar furry shadow and she begins to leap into the air. He bends to put on his shoes, trying to avoid her pounces as she is ramping up to go for her morning walk. Shoes, check.

"Go get my sweater," Dad says to Peaches. She runs up the stairs and returns with a sweater slightly damp with dog drool he purposefully leaves on the floor for her. The hours of training come to life and he puts on the carefully mouthed sweater. Sweater, check. Ball, check. Turn on her collar light, check. It is only 6:15 a.m. and it's September, so it's still dark outside.

I hear the front door close. They will complete their walk, wipe off some muddy paws, and Dad will drive off leaving me and Peaches to our day. I turn back to my coffee and I am surprised when I hear the front door open again. I turn to see Dad's face. It looks tight in places and yet slack too. He is shaking. He squeaks out, "Peaches," in a frantic plea, and I leap up from my chair.

"Did she get hit by a car?" I say.

"No, I need help," he huffs through tight breaths.

I can feel the adrenaline rush through my body. My brain switches from emotion to motion and I put on my shoes. He is running down the alley into the darkness. He yells, "Get the van."

I hate driving our van. It is so big, like a bus. Everything slows down. It takes forever for the go light to turn on as I wait for the diesel engine to warm. The seat won't click into place as I jerk it forward so my feet will reach the pedals. The alley is directly across from our driveway, and I finally drive 40 metres into the dark and see him on his knees beside her. I put it in park and leave it running. I hop out.

Peaches is panting. She is lying on her side next to a short fence post. She isn't getting up, but she is alive. Her collar is lying by her head near the fence post and her bowels seem to have let go. Dad is kneeling over her making unrecognizable mewling sounds to her, and he is crying. He stands up and opens the side door of the van and closes it again. He changes his mind.

He says, "You drive, I will hold her."

It is still only 6:20 a.m. Our vet won't be open. I know there is an animal hospital nearby as I have seen its lit sign from the main thoroughfare through town. I think to go there.

He lifts her up as best as he can and gets in. She is lying across his lap and she is still panting heavily. Her eyes are not the reassuring brown like usual; they are black and scared. I try not to think too much because I know I have to drive.

"She's going to die," Dad squeaks out at some point in the drive. It's as though all that tightness has made it nearly impossible for him to speak. But there is anger and fear in it. I can see his tears falling onto Peaches's soft golden fur. But I drive. I pull up to the front doors of the animal hospital and let them get out together. I quickly park and head inside.

Dad and the reception nurse are trying to talk, but he is holding Peaches so I step forward and let my adrenaline speak for me.

"She was playing ball and ran into a post. Please help us," I say.

Dad and the nurse disappear behind the sterile doors and then Dad is back. He comes and sits beside me leadened. I am filling out some form. He is still crying and he turns to me.

"She is going to die. I know it," he says.

A young doctor comes out from the back. She looks grave and is shaking her head. She says something about doing a test and that there is no feeling in her limbs. Her back is broken. She should be put down now. We know. We knew it from the moment it happened.

Lumps rise in my throat and sadness sighs out of me in huffs. This is going to be goodbye. She is only a puppy. Only two. Only wanting to play in the morning. Only wanting to be a good companion. Only wanting to be part of our hearts. Mine is breaking.

We go into the back of the hospital. She is lying on a couch wrapped in a blanket. I know what is coming. Dad buries his face in her fur and gently pets her.

"You are such a good girl," he says. I choke on my tears. He loves her so much. His emotion is raw and unbearable. It is rare for him to display any, and I can hardly stand to see his grief.

Between gulps of air and hugs and hiccups we watch her go. He gives her permission. He tells her she is a good girl. He releases her.

This is not supposed to be how the story goes. She is only a puppy. And we will never know exactly what happened. Did she jump for the ball and come down on the post? Did her collar get caught and swing her around into the post? All Dad knows is he threw the ball like any other morning—like 500 other mornings—into the dark and he heard a yelp and a small thud. It was a morning like any other morning, but then it wasn't.

We drive home and wake you up to tell you. You are so angry and hurt. "Why didn't you wake me before?" you ask. It all happened so fast, so early, so unexpectedly. You are not a morning person. You would have slowed our trip to the hospital. How did we know that it wouldn't have mattered how fast we arrived? We are all crying at this loss and fight off the anger. We all want answers and someone to blame.

"I'm sorry you didn't get a chance to say goodbye to her," I say.

"I never want another dog," you sniff.

I know the pain of this loss is hard for you. She brought us an unconditional love that is so rare in this world and I hope you will find space for more puppy love again in the future.

Being Fully Invested Is the Best Choice
Cody, age 6. Me, age 29.

The summer sun is warming the deck we are sitting on. The condensation from our glasses forms pools of water on the glass tabletop. I sip my iced tea and wipe my damp hand on my shorts. Grandma and Grandpa are talking about work and you are poking a stick in between the deck boards. You look at me and sigh. It is hot and you are bored. Visiting Grandma and Grandpa can be tough for a six-year-old. You don't want to sit and listen to us talk and you are tired of watching the few kids movies they have.

"Hey Cody, why don't you play catch with the dog for a few minutes?" I suggest.

You grab a ball to play fetch with our dog Dusty and head down the gravel laneway to play. I watch you throw the ball a few times and then Dusty lies down in the shade, refusing to retrieve it in the hot sun. You play catch with yourself and I turn away. I need to go to the bathroom.

I come back and see that Dad and Grandma and Grandpa are around the side of the house looking at something in the garden. I scan the lane for you and I don't see you playing there anymore.

"Hey Schaene, where's Cody?" I ask, trying to sound calm.

"He's playing ball with the dog," he says and turns to look where you should have been.

The lane ends in a swale. It is a tall-grassed swampy section of land between a few farms. The grass is taller than you. I run down the gravel laneway and look behind the garage on my way. You are nowhere to be seen. I stand at the edge of the swale and yell your name but the

69

wind is rustling through the grass making my voice fade into nothingness.

There is a wind coursing through me too. I am filled with images of you knee deep in mud struggling to free yourself. I see you fall forward into some water and thrash to breathe. You cannot swim yet. Why haven't we taught you to swim? I imagine the search party we will have to assemble. I imagine the darkness coming and your little chin quivering as the night closes in and you get cold. I am being buffeted around by the gales of thoughts and I can't get my bearings. Dad, Grandpa, and Grandma all come to the edge of the swale to look for you too. Dad heads into the swale. There is more yelling and more stomping around in the grass and mud. Minutes pass. I think terrible thoughts: "I knew I should not have loved you with my whole heart. I should have closed myself off more so the pain of loss would not be so great. I cannot lose you. This is not happening."

And then I see it: a ball being thrown up into the air again and again from the middle of the swamp. You are showing us where you are. You bright boy. You smart boy. You alive boy. And in that moment I unbox my heart again, but a little piece stays hidden inside. It is safer in there. I cannot expose all of me to this danger. I cannot be all in. This love is unsafe. I am only asking for loss, and heartbreak, and grief.

You come out of the swamp with mud up to your knees and a wide grin.

"Cody, you need to tell us where you are going. You can't be going into the swamp alone," I bark at you.

"I was just on an adventure, Mom," you reply innocently.

I wrap my arms around you and think about the possible loss. You are only six. How many more times will there be when I might lose you? Can I love you "all in" or should I withhold some of me? You childhood is already passing so fast, but I don't know if I can withstand the daily fears of you out in this dangerous world. When I am boxed up,

70

I miss things. The fear of letting go or losing you makes me not want to love you with my whole heart.

And yet, isn't that the whole point? To have the deepest, most loving, and most vibrant relationships, despite the possibility of loss? If I don't open my heart fully to you, how can you learn to love fully? I don't want to end up at the end of my life realizing that love is all life is anyway. But it is hard. As my parents are aging, I am finding myself resistant to visiting, resistant to sharing long phone calls with them, and resistant to fully investing myself in them. I know they will leave me, and the closer I am to them, the more difficult the goodbye will be. But what do I have in this life but these feelings?

Even in those relationships that I know will not be long or fruitful, I must bring my whole self to them and bring love to them. It colours in the spaces and brings life to the moments. It raises my spirits and brings comfort to others. It is my real work on this planet and I should not shy away from it, for it is the only thing that will sustain me. I just pray I don't lose you because I don't know if I could bear it.

Make Sure You Play the Field

Me, looking back.

I am 16 and taking the risk of asking a boy to go out with me. I didn't want to hear it, but I couldn't stop him from saying it. "Well, I umm … Kirsten, you are the kind of girl boys marry, not the kind of girl boys date." My heart breaks. I have been crushing on him for so long, and he is rejecting me. I am his friend, nothing more. I am the beige kind of girl. A colourless companion who tags along until marrying age and then suddenly becomes the perfect shade of wife, chaste and pure. Other girls swing from partner to partner like in a ballroom dance, swept up in the tide of young love, while I watch from the sidelines. But the boys aren't entirely to blame.

I'm not especially good-looking and I am certainly conservative. I am uncomfortable in my skin and don't want much of it to show. When my friends giggle and share their encounters with boys, I feel naive and out of the loop. How do they know these things? Where and when do these things happen? My sexuality can't exactly grow in the darkness, without the light of lust shining on it. I pour myself into my studies and wait.

Dad and I have known each other a long time. We were friends and hung around the same people for much of our childhood and teenage years. I didn't think of Dad in any way beyond friendship until grade 13. I suppose then that I suddenly became that perfect shade of wife. So we dated and married. I had a few other boyfriends before then, but they were young loves without much physical intimacy. You can probably guess that he was my first and only.

How wonderful to have had only one lover—the church and traditionalists must be so proud! And when I took my wedding vows, I meant them. For me marriage is a commitment to one person. For life.

That's a long time. I love Dad dearly, but there is a part of me that is, how do I say this, curious. He is a more than adequate lover, but yet, how would I know? I don't have any comparison. It is an itch I cannot scratch. I don't think about it often, but in 24 years of marriage, it has had time to bubble up here and there. It is not a strong enough curiosity for me to cheat on Dad, but it feels a little like I missed out on something.

This is probably not the advice most mothers would give their sons, but I want you to make sure you play the field. This is not permission to be reckless with yourself or others. That's not healthy either. Instead I want you to appreciate women, in all their variations. Date lots, meet lots of different kinds of women, and love some of those women. At least a few. I want you to know what is out there. I want you to know with certainty what you are choosing. I want you to be able to commit and never wonder like I wonder.

You Can Marry Anyone

Me, looking back.

Like most little girls raised in this culture, I had fantasies about the man I would marry. I don't remember seeing a specific guy in my head. Instead he had certain qualities and he made me feel a certain way. He was loving and provided for our family, and he made me feel like the most important person in his life. Great fantasy. Maybe you have had a fantasy about your perfect wife too. Does she look a certain way or does she make you feel great about yourself? Dad has lived up to my fantasy, but what if he hadn't?

I'm not sure what your impression is of our marriage. I know you have formed one though, just like I formed one about Grandma and Grandpa's marriage. What I saw growing up helped me form my image of the perfect marriage, either by good examples or bad examples of those around me. There were things I wanted from a marriage, like an equal partner and someone I could talk to who respected my thoughts. From our point of view, Dad and I have that working partnership. We both cook, we both clean, we both work, and we both shared the parenting. We try to demonstrate respectful ways to disagree and how to collaborate to solve a problem. Maybe you see that we did this well or maybe not, but I am sure your vision of an ideal marriage will be formed from our mistakes and successes.

So here is the thing: it really doesn't matter who you marry. Dad could have met all the criteria for my perfect man and our marriage could have failed. A fantasy is not a marriage. What you saw in our marriage was from working together over time and forming that relationship. You could essentially marry anyone! Pick some person at random and perform the ceremony. It is not critical that you have those butterflies in your belly or that you pine away at night knowing that she completes you. You could marry someone you didn't even meet until your wedding day. There is one ingredient that a marriage needs, and a fantasy or even familiarity is not it.

I don't come from a culture of arranged marriages, but I believe that dating is not the safeguard you need for a successful marriage. Dating might be fun and send sparks of electricity through you, but that wears off quickly. What a marriage needs is love, and love is not electric sparks. Love is commitment. Warm, respectful, unwavering commitment. And it is two-sided. A marriage needs two people who are committed to making the marriage work. That's it. It seems so simple and yet it is missing from so many marriages.

Marriage is long. We've been married longer than you have been alive, so it's probably hard for you to imagine the length of that commitment. To one person. Every day. It hasn't all been perfect either. What you see is practiced and honed and refined through years of working at it. Dad and I had our tough years, just like most people. He changed and I changed. He certainly isn't the man I married and I am not the woman he married either.

On our wedding day this is who we were: I was a budding biologist certain I was going to work in science and Dad was in business school. We had plans of living in a sustainable house, having two kids, a farm, and travelling the world. Twenty-four years later, this is how that played out: I never worked in biology except during university, Dad never became a business man (at least not in the suit and tie way), we don't have a sustainable house or farm, have only one child, and have only been to a handful of countries. Those differences are just the tangible ones. I have changed on the inside and Dad has too.

Neither of you stays the same (and I wouldn't want you to). Every day you have to make a choice to love your partner for the person they are today. If you both make this choice, then your marriage ticks along. That is the commitment: both of you choosing to love the person for who they are. And so I believe it would be true if you were to marry just anyone. They won't stay the same person you married and you won't either. All it takes is the commitment to love the person for who they are right now.

It is hard to love someone who changes. Throughout our marriage I have probably wasted more time and energy than I care to admit on wanting Dad to be different. I am an extrovert and Dad is an introvert. I think by talking out loud and Dad processes things quietly. I don't worry so much about how many words I use to say something and Dad thinks carefully about each word chosen. We couldn't be more different in these ways (and in many more) and it can bring up many challenges. We argue differently, we manage stress differently, and we communicate on every level differently. I used to fight hard to get him to see things and do things my way. And yes, you can judge me for that. It is hard to let go of wanting someone to be different. There are still times that I struggle with this. But is so unfair of me to ask him to be someone he is not, especially since I know how hurtful it is when someone asks me to do the same.

It took a lot of years to realize that no matter how much time I spent thinking about how Dad could be different, he didn't change. Instead my perception of him became more blown out of proportion. Instead of seeing him as he was, I saw him more and more as he wasn't. In that clouded perception, I began to miss his gifts and talents. I began to ignore the beauty of his personality, and I missed his perfection just as he was.

It is so much easier to break this commitment than to work at love. You can see examples all around you. Some people simply have an affair, or continue to believe that someone else should fulfil them and bring them happiness. This is the hallmark of our current society and it plays out in the number of divorces we see. I do think there are reasons to end a marriage, infidelity and abuse, but so often people choose to end their marriages just because it got hard. It gets hard when one partner lets go of the commitment.

So I suppose I'm not saying anything new. It is the same message we have heard about all relationships; you have to accept people for who they are. The trouble is that it is one of the hardest things to do. Your commitment to your marriage, to marrying anyone, comes with the responsibility to love the person for who they are. There is freedom to choose anyone, but in that choice, you assume the responsibility of accepting who you have chosen.

You could marry anyone, because it takes the same skills as marrying someone who you think is your "soulmate." Acceptance and commitment. There is no need to worry about whether you find that "right" person; instead, find someone who is as committed as you are to making things work.

Love What Is

Me, looking back.

It would be comical if someone followed Dad and I around and recorded our conversations. I natter away with an unending stream of noise and Dad interjects a word or two here or there. I wonder sometimes if he thinks he has been allotted a finite number of words for his lifetime and doesn't want to use up too many too soon. They say opposites attract, and some might even say that Dad couldn't get a word in edgewise if he tried, but this has been one of the bigger hurdles in our marriage.

I want Dad to talk more. I thought a marriage would include long, deep conversations, remember that fantasy? I also thought my spouse would be a sounding board and strategic partner. I need Dad's input sometimes, and he doesn't always have the words to give me. I've wished for him to be different. I've begged him to talk more. I've even yelled at him to change. There is a hole where his thoughts should be. I want to hear him ramble, but it just isn't to be.

That might seem small to someone else, a spouse that doesn't talk much. But it is a big deal to me. After 24 years of marriage (to date), I am finally figuring out that I need to love Dad for who he is, just as he is. Pensive and quiet. It seems so easy to say and so obvious, but accepting this is one of the hardest things I've had to do. When I need a good listener I can go to Dad, but when I need an adviser or a thought partner, I am finally learning that I need to go elsewhere for that. Why did I think that Dad should fill every role I need filled? Why did it take me so long and so much heartache to learn this?

"Loving someone for who they are" is far deeper than that simple phrase. It means that every time Dad reacts to something in a way I wouldn't, I need to love him for that. It means that when I need him to be more talkative and he isn't, I need to love him for that. It means that when he cuts the onions his way, packs the groceries his way, drives the car his way, I need to love him for that. It seems so difficult because loving those things that are different is accepting them but also holding them up as strengths. Often, they are also my weaknesses. His differences point right at what I am not good at. No wonder it is so hard for me to love him as he is! I am looking right at things about myself that I might not love.

That is the point. Our relationships are mirrors to not only see our own strengths but to see our weaknesses and to embrace them, in all their messiness. Every time our "corners" get in the way, I see my own strengths and weaknesses. Dad sees his too. I like to think about it like river stones. We rub up against each other when the tough current of life moves over us, and eventually our rough edges are ground down by each other until we are smooth. He is polishing me and I am polishing him. My loving him as he is allows me to love me as I am. He is also able to love me as I am, and love himself too!

The polishing through our relationship rubs a little bit of him off on me along the way. Loving Dad as he is leaves me open and receptive. I am able to learn from him and use his strengths to help me grow, but I can't do that when I am blinded by frustration and anger. Each time I am able to witness his response to something, a little of him rubs off on me. My favorite example is his ability to go with the flow. I have learned to not plan as much for vacations from Dad. What a gift that has been.

I have learned that I cannot change Dad; he changes on his own. It is my role to love him as he is, because it allows him to love himself. It also reminds me to embrace his unique combination of personality traits and in turn embrace my own.

It Is Hard to Be Married a Long Time

Cody, age 21. Me, age 44.

The alarm goes off at 4:30 a.m. It is such an unnatural, jarring sound. I push the button to stop it and begin rationalizing how I could quit my job, how I could call in sick, how I could do anything but swing my feet out of bed and get my day started. But I know I have to go. I grab a housecoat and stumble into the bathroom. I take care of my morning routine—shower, hair, teeth, clothes, coffee—and think about my day. I will be riding the bus into downtown at 6:00 a.m. and won't be home again until 5:00 p.m. At 5:45 a.m. I head back up to our bedroom to wake up Dad. I am his alarm clock with a kiss on the forehead and a gentle rub of his arm. He silently reaches out and squeezes my hand good morning. I head back downstairs. I pack my lunch, computer, and phone. I dig around in my wallet for a bus ticket and run through the mental checklist of stuff I need for the day. I have everything. I will have time to do a little writing when I arrive at the office building where I work. I will also have a bit of time to do some reading while I ride the bus. Multitasking, planning, and productivity are such a part of me. I am always thinking of ways to maximize my life.

I watch the clock, self-absorbed in my to-do list, and pop up from my seat at 6:00 a.m. to put my shoes on. I can hear Dad finishing his morning routine upstairs. I get my gear together: backpack, light jacket instead of parka today, mitts, and bus ticket. Dad comes down the stairs with a stampede of blonde fur. Sunny, our golden retriever, wishes me good morning with a bit of a parade and a stolen kiss on the hand. Dad waits while I zip up my jacket. He looks right into my eyes like a little kid. Impatient but patient. He is putting on his most bright-eyed face this morning, even though he isn't much of a morning person. Once I get my coat zipped, his arms envelop me.

81

It could have been a quick blown kiss. It could simply have been a "Have a good day" yelled from the kitchen while he poured his coffee, but instead it is a hug. It isn't a quick hug; it is long and slow. His hug brings me back from my head and into my body again. His hug reminds me we are parting and I sense he wants a piece of closeness to take with him for his day. I am present in his arms this morning. I am aware we are together and reminded of our partnership. We could have missed this if he hadn't been intentional about slowing down. It would have been lost in the obligatory send off.

We can get so busy. So wrapped up in our own lives. I worked with Dad for many years, and we saw each other every day, all day. But now we are working apart and it takes a lot of brain space to manage our business lives. I live in my head so much. I have an entire life in there with plans and dreams and observations. It is colourful and mesmerizing. So much so that I escape into my head and forget my body is attached and that I am living in this world.

It's so simple to slip into routine. Dad and I have been there. Days string together like uniform plastic beads. Sameness, repetition, striving, working. It is so easy to be lulled to sleep into a flat life. Combined with my tendency to live in my head, this averageness is poisonous. I have easily taken Dad for granted. As unnoticed as the other plastic parts of my day. A Ken doll that Barbie sends off to work in the morning before she gets on with the real part of her day. Her own story. But Dad is so good at being present. He lives in his body and less in his head. He is my grounding force and forces me to remember him. In remembering him, I remember myself. I find my body again. I return to earth and I see things around me.

Dad and I have learned to recognize the signs that it is time to fall in love again. Weeks go by without more than a surface conversation: how was work, what are we doing this weekend, what is on the grocery list, and what renovations are we doing this summer. These are not the conversations that will hold us together. So we book a weekend downtown or go on vacation or simply reinstate "date breakfasts." We find a way to get past the daily routine and see each other again. We look back into each other's eyes to see our souls, not just our bodies. The conversation might deepen with talk about fulfilment and dreams or fears and expectations, but sometimes it is just reconnecting to the undercurrent of our hearts and knowing that we are moving in unison again.

The flat parts make us forget each other and take each other for granted. When there are lots of exciting things going on, it is easy to find yourself and to share with the other person. These peaks and valleys provide enough contrast for you to find yourself. It is the prairies that are a wasteland of monotony. It is these flat parts that are the peril to love.

What the Bedroom Is For

Cody, less than a year old. Me, age 23.

You are finally tucked in for the night. I don't have anything left, and I feel an angry exhaustion come over me. I want to be in bed sleeping. Why can't I be in bed sleeping? Who is to blame?! Today was breastfeeding, diapers, toys, dinner, crying, walking, cuddling, soothing from one bleary-eyed minute to the next. I sneak out of your bedroom and pull the door almost closed. I know you will only be down for a few hours and I need to get some sleep. I head into the bedroom and crawl into my side. Dad is already in bed reading by the lamp on his nightstand. He rolls over and looks at me. I can see he wants to help, but how can he do that when you just want to be breastfed?

He puts his hand on my shoulder to let me know he understands, but how can he? The fury foams so fast I can't stop it and I push his hand away.

"You just don't understand!" I say. "You get to leave all day. I can't escape like you can and I'm so lonely. He is up all night. I need to get more sleep. I can't even have a shower. You don't get it!" The blame comes out in a wave. I lay on my back and stare at the ceiling while the hot tears flow past my ears into the pillow. I shut Dad out and roll over to sleep in a stone-cold bed with a blanket of anger around me.

You wake me up a few hours later. My eyes are swollen from crying and a lack of sleep. I make my way through the tainted fog to climb back into bed. Even the morning light is not enough to burn it off.

A few days later I am standing in the kitchen trying to get dinner made while you crawl around at my feet. I hear Dad drive up and then walk through the back door. He kisses the back of my neck and bends down and sweeps you up off the floor. He throws you onto his hip and takes the spoon out of my hand.

"Go and take a shower," he says. "I've got this."

I can't believe how good the warm water feels falling over me. I have been rushing my showers while you cried in your bouncy chair, even though I kept the curtain open so you could see me. I can hear you fussing but I stick my head under the warm water and let it drown out the sound. I feel new and fresh. I feel ready for another long night.

Dad serves up my plate and tells me to go eat. I haven't eaten a meal while it was still hot in so long. You are usually so fussy that I can only get a few bites in and it gets cold while I soothe you. Dad is doing what he can. I feel so guilty for yelling at him a few days ago. I was so tired and it wasn't his fault. I shouldn't have attempted to talk about anything when I was tired and at my wits' end. No good can come from a conversation held late at night and wrought with emotion. I should have left it for a better time.

"I'm sorry for being so angry the other night," I say remorsefully.

"I know how hard this is," Dad says. "But let's make a deal, okay?"

"What's that?" I ask.

"Let's promise not to talk about anything important in our bedroom, okay?" he says timidly.

"But it's the only time we have alone together," I reason.

"We will just have to work to find a better time," he assures me.

He's right. The bedroom is no place for emotionally charged personal conversations. It is a sacred place that should be safe, free from baggage, and quiet. We are figuring this stuff out the hard way, but we are figuring it out. I finish my dinner and take you from Dad while he heads to the kitchen to get his dinner.

Getting Through

Me, looking back.

Dad and I were the best couple. We had figured it all out. We knew the give and take necessary to make it work. We were focused on allowing each other to grow and change. We chose love, communicated well, and topped up our happiness from each other instead of relying on the other to provide our happiness.

But it wasn't enough. Our arrogance only assured us those first seven or so years. We managed to get through the money troubles of early coupledom, having children, and beginning careers. Statistics suggest your own marriage will fail at this point. It does for many people, and it could have for us too.

It was an uphill battle to get past the circling and role playing of the first few years to find honest communication. It was hard to get past the daily frustrations of dealing with someone else's stuff and habits to finally appreciating having someone else in our space. And it took many years to get to the place of just knowing what the other person is feeling and thinking without talking.

Latch onto that arrogance in the first few years. It builds up your resolve to stick it out when the first tides and waves rock your relationship. Let history be the safe harbour you can return to when the seas get rough.

Dad and I were arrogant and sure about our marriage. We fell together peacefully like we fell into our bed each night. Nobody warned us about the boredom that comes after you finally get through the first few years of creating a home, family, and career. Once you start to tread water in the world, things take a different shape. Boredom, familiarity, and the never-ending grind takes its toll. I looked at Dad wanting him to be the spark in this dullness. I was looking for adventure and newness and he was looking at me for the same. But neither of us could really provide that for someone else. We had to learn that we were both responsible for our excitement and happiness. It is too much of a burden to place on someone else.

Even mastering our own senses of adventure did not make us immune to the possibility of growing apart. I'd hazard to say that there is no solution for marriage or any way to create a sure method of securing the commitment across your life. Things change, new scenarios come up, moods and personalities evolve. The benefit of a long time together means the history can become the foundation from which you navigate back to love again. And it is about falling in love again and again. Being in love every minute of every day is not sustainable. It is nearly impossible. Dad and I have been in and out of love throughout our marriage, but we have kept our commitment. Sometimes only because of our history.

We needed communication skills too. We learned many of those the hard way. Dad isn't a big talker and I won't let him get a word in. We have learned to listen as much as we talk. We listen for the in-between stuff, the stuff that isn't said. It is much easier to do that after 23 years, because we know each other so intimately. We know facial expressions, body language, and what a pause might mean. The listening also means we have learned to reflect the other person's thoughts back to them through clarifying questions and a demonstration of understanding.

We have made it 23 years, but we still struggle. Dad still likes to solve my problems with advice and solutions instead of just validating my feelings. I still struggle with how little he shares as an introvert. But we know this about each other and have learned to accept these differences.

All I can hope for you is that you will let your arrogance get your through the first few years of marriage, then lean hard on your history. Work hard to build the communication necessary to see it all through, and fall back into love again and again.

Hurdles and Forgiveness

Me, looking back.

I cannot tell you what the hurdles of your marriage will be. Ours were not expected. In fact, our hurdles were things I never saw coming or could have ever imagined. But know that the hurdles will come and you will need to be patient with your relationship while you find a new rhythm. I think more than once Dad and I were only "roommates" while we worked to fall back in love. But roommates was still a better solution than destroying our family.

At the beginning, we had talked through the things we believed in and the things we felt passionate about. I could anticipate the things that Dad would agree with and the things he would reject. I knew what he might order from a menu, how he would handle a customer situation, and where he would like to go on vacation. These choices made tiny shifts over time (we all evolve over 24 years), and I adjusted my knowledge of him as he changed. But the fundamental person did not change. I am sure it was the same for him.

For Dad's stag party, I asked only one thing: that he not go to the strippers. I have some pretty strong feelings about that industry and pornography, and didn't want that to be part of the beginning of our life together. I am sure attendees to his stag were a bit disappointed, but I think Dad respected my wishes. We were laying the groundwork for trust and respect and he knew what this meant to me.

Sex is such an intimate, self-esteem-filled exchange for me. It may not be for everyone, but it is for me. I have never been promiscuous, as I could not "bare myself" fully to another person unless I felt completely safe and in love. That high standard of trust and love would be tarnished if I invited someone else into the experience. I did not want any other images in my partner's mind, especially ones that come from porn.

Porn is unfeeling. It really is all about the act and none of the other things associated with sharing this experience with someone. There is no intimacy, no love. It is merely a couple of bodies engaged in the act with some terrible plot line of how they got there. I hardly imagine having sex with my pizza delivery guy. Perhaps this makes me a prude, but I doubt I am alone.

Thinking that my partner has filled his mind with image after image of sexual acts with no feeling does not make me feel comfortable and safe. What sort of partner will he be? Attentive, loving, emotionally connected—I don't think so.

I wanted the most intimate experience two loving partners can share to be a safe, trusting, and beautiful experience. It was no secret I felt this way, and one of the first beliefs I shared with Dad.

So when he violated it, what was I to feel? How could someone you love knowingly do something that would hurt you to the core? My trust was shaken. Isn't trust knowing that the other person will not intentionally hurt you? When that hurt comes, how can you heal the wound and not continually poke at the scar and relive the pain?

I don't know how I did it. I was crazy at first. I tore through all our records and papers and computers looking to find if they hid anything else unimaginable. Was anything I thought to be true, true? I tried to return to routine. The restraint of not looking through more phone bills was so hard. I stuffed down the compulsion to read every email and look through the entire internet search history. I faked normalcy. I thought if I could just hold up my end of the usual dance, we would return to flow, right?

You see those people in movies that are overcome with grief and hurt. They act irrationally, pulling at their hair and bodies. Pacing a room, walking and mumbling, and making no sense. They seem possessed, and then they collapse like rag dolls and melt into tears and gripping sobs. I've been through exactly that. My body was trying to reconcile the fight-or-flight response on a level you cannot imagine. It would have been easier if there had been an enemy to combat in front of me, but the opponent was my own paradigm. The world view I had constructed was ripped away, and I was looking behind the curtain at a world I didn't know existed.

I would have crawled out of my own body if I could. I would take one step forward into accepting this new reality and then retreat again into my old paradigm, only to find that I could see through its thin, gauzy facade. Each step into the new reality was painful and terribly uncertain. It wasn't the betrayal that was so hard to manage. It was the disorientation that comes from realizing you were duped.

I am sure everyone heals in different ways. I don't hold things against Dad anymore. I do have fleeting moments when I wonder if he will hurt me again, but for the most part I have moved on and we have rebuilt trust.

Forgiveness and trust are long roads to rebuild. It is now many years later, and I can say with certainty that I can look back at that time and know that I am healed. In fact, our marriage grew enormously because of this hurdle. Who was I to ask Dad to believe what I believe, but equally, who was Dad to ask me to set aside my beliefs? You will find yourself here; most marriages have hurdles such as this. But it is never the things you imagine, and the solutions are the hardest to navigate.

Where Intimacy Begins

Me, looking back.

I have always worn my heart on my sleeve. I can remember being inconsolable at about four or five after watching *Charlotte's Web*. I think my Mom let me sleep in their bed. I was such a sensitive kid. It was awkward and got in the way sometimes. There was no way to stop the feelings from pouring out, and in public, it was beyond embarrassing. I remember trying to bite my lip and think of other things and stuff down the giant lump forming in my throat while watching *Old Yeller* in grade seven. It really was an inconvenience and an insult to my ego to cry openly in front of all my dry-eyed friends. There was giggling and pointing at my softness. Not only was my body soft, but my insides were too. Softness is rejected, ridiculed, and wrong.

But I no longer regret it. I choose not to go and see heart-wrenching movies in public theatres—thank God for Netflix. But I don't try to stop the tears when they come. Trying to hold them back is a bit like trying to swallow your own vomit. It burns your throat, sickens your stomach, and makes you feel a bit dead inside. Now I let them leak out unhindered, and it is better that way. It is embracing the range of emotions we get to experience, as life is simply moments of poignant emotion. Without those punctuations, we live a flat life and cannot remember what happened to us. Our emotions create memory, and my soft memories are some of the best ones.

My softness has made me a connector and a lover. There is a difficult side to being this way. I struggle when I am surrounded by those who do not think of love, empathy, and sympathy, who are closed off inside their shells with armoured eyes and hearts. This can be a source of longing and discontent. The connectors and the lovers in families know that without us, many of the memories would not be made, and the chasms between us would be unbridged and the silences unbroken. It is lonely and tiring work to dig through the layers of protection to find another's soul and bring them along by the hand to the edge of discomfort where intimacy begins.

I want the whole world to open their eyes and their hearts to what is important. Love, giving, sharing, and trying. These are the electric activities. The sparks of life. Creation. But I also know how hard it is for many people, like you and Dad. You are uncomfortable with those feelings because your vulnerability is too fresh. If it gets exposed, you might just get swallowed up by it. It might just expand in the light and never fit back into its box. I mean, how can you or any other male in our society step into the predestined role of man, provider, strong shoulder, if you cry at sappy movies? And so, you put on armour: a condescending laugh at the sappy movie, a quiet shrug of your shoulders instead of a response, or a set of your jaw to steel yourself. It is your shield from letting the tears flow. It is your distraction while you swallow the bile rising in your throat. But I am not fooled, because I have tried to use those tactics too. Except, for me, it is something I never mastered, and I'm not sorry.

Dad is letting his tears out more too. I don't know why that seems to change the older men get. Is it because they become tired of holding everything inside? Is it because they too don't like the taste of vomit? And even though most of us are pretty unattractive when we cry, it is beautiful to see him cry. There is a humanness to it. I look across at him and see a man who has a heart, who embraces his softness, and who relates to joy and pain and sorrow openly.

I hope that one day you too will let a movie or story move you. I promise you won't crumble. I promise it actually opens up more strength. It gives you practice for those soft moments in your own life— the birth of a child, the loss of a friend, the overwhelming moments of gratitude you can find in the everyday. It is the beginning of intimacy and living in a deeper way.

SECTION 4: WITH REGRET

Regret Comes Disguised as Decision

Cody, not yet born. Me, age 18.

It's the end of school, my last few days of high school ever. I am flying high, top of my class in so many areas and ready for so much more. I am packing to move to the University of Guelph for a summer position under a wildlife biology professor. I am excited and terrified. I can hardly wait to get out of my parents' house, but this means stepping into the unknown, and I'm nervous. I think a little bit about missing out on my graduation ceremony but I am heading out on an adventure and I couldn't ask this professor to wait to hire me. I quickly erase those thoughts and zip up my suitcase.

My parents drive me to Southern Ontario and drop me off at the university. I find my dorm room. I meet my roommates and I start my job. My professor is fun, and what is even more exciting is that he doesn't tell me what to do. He asks me what I think I should do. I am so happy planning an experiment, designing the infrastructure, running trials, participating in bird tagging, that I forget about home and what is happening there without me.

I have no instant updates from friends or family because the long-distance phone calls are too hard to schedule or pay for. I can't share my daily struggles or excitement. I feel like I'm living in my own bubble. My roommates and professor are the only contact I have, and sometimes it's a few days between talking to even them. But I am happy. I have successfully begun my life. I am out of my parents' home and forging my own path on the way to adulthood.

I don't really think too much about missing my high school graduation, and I have no one around who reminds me of home. As one of the top students in my school, there will be awards and certificates, scholarships and accolades, that I will receive. I am already at my new job and, really, who cares about a high school graduation in the bigger scheme of things, right?

My job wraps up and I start university that fall. It is hard. I am a small fish in a big pond, and I am struggling. I never had to work this hard in high school. I think about what it was like to be top of my class in so many courses. I had studied, I had reviewed, and I had crammed. And it paid off—I had excelled. My average grade was 93 percent in all my grade 13 classes. Impressive, but empty. And even more empty was never actually getting the recognition from my peers for all that work.

It seems petty. Surely, a high school graduation is not my pinnacle of success? Surely there will be other achievements, greater achievements, worth celebrating?

What if I am never top of anything after high school? I regret that I didn't take a few moments to really soak up some applause. Skipping my high school graduation is likely not something anyone thought I would regret. The decision to go to a job over a graduation ceremony seems pretty cut and dried. It is only now that I look back and realize I regret that decision.

As you head through life, just know that you might not be able to prevent regrets. You cannot see what will lead to them. You will be making decisions all the way along, with your best interests at heart. You will be seizing opportunities and saying no to one path at the fork in the road. Sometimes we wish we had veered right when we veered left, but there is no way to know that in advance. They come disguised as decisions, and you make the best ones you can with the information you have. It is only afterward that you can see them more clearly and the burden they have brought you.

You Have to Play the Game, but You Don't Have to Like It

Cody, age 12. Me, age 35.

"Do you have any homework?" I ask. I already know the answer because your teacher called me today to tell me you haven't been doing any of the assignments in math.

"No," you say, pouting, and start to move toward the stairs to go to your room.

"Really? I think you do. How 'bout some math?" I ask as I follow you up the stairs.

"Maybe. But I know the stuff, Mom. It's so easy," you say, looking defiant and defeated at the same time. You flop onto the bed.

"I know you are smart, but your teacher needs to see that. Your assignments are not so much about learning the material but showing her you know it. It's a game," I explain, grasping for a way to convince you.

"A game?" you ask, looking up at me.

"All of this is a game," I say, waving my arms in an encompassing circle. "The world is set up as a giant game. School is a game; you do the assignment, get a grade, pass a class, and graduate. Then you start the work game—get a beginner job, get promoted, pour your life into work, and then retire. It's how our world is set up. It is a game we all have to play, but you don't have to like it."

Your eyes widen. You can feel the futility of this aspect of our society that I am sharing with you. I shouldn't have told you so young, but I am so tired of having this fight about homework.

"Is there another way?" you ask searchingly.

"Not really." I sigh and watch your face go slack. You are too young to know this.

What is a flummoxed mom supposed to do? I am tired of the nightly battles with you to do homework. I am tired of the frustrated conversations with teachers who know you are bright enough but can't understand your reluctance to do assignments. And I am tired of everyone walking around the elephant that is sitting in the room. I chose to talk about the elephant.

So you're ruined. You can no longer see any of the hoops and hurdles as anything more than a game. You can no longer view the pursuit of a title and a promotion as anything more than a game. And I know you don't like it now and I worry how you will feel in the future. I see you trying to decide if you can find a way to not play this game. You are struggling with the meaninglessness of it all. I should have left the curtain down. I should have left it all as a mystery. How will you play the game now without be jaded? How will you find the energy each day to act out your role on this stage and not feel phony? How will you be able to deal with the perspective of puppet and master? You are here on the outside with me. I know what it is like to stand outside society, and it is harder to be on the outside.

You Think There Is Time

Cody, age 10. Me, age 33.

I put the suitcase into the trunk. We are wrapping up the last visit to camp before we move to Calgary. You are glued to your Gameboy on the couch and Grandma is puttering in the kitchen. No one is talking much. Dad slams the trunk shut and we walk back into the camp to pry you from your cozy perch and make the drive out of the bush.

"Come on, Cody, it's time to go," I say to you. "Got your Gameboy and shoes?"

You climb off the couch oblivious to the momentousness of these next few minutes.

Grandpa grabs your hand; you are his little buddy. My mind flashes to memories of Grandpa and you playing with Tonka trucks on the road, Grandpa down in the grass immersed in your imaginary world, and Grandpa telling you stories and reading to you. He let down his guard with you and loved you more than I have seen him love anyone else. He slowed for you. He saw you. In your childhood he was all the things I wanted from him when I was little.

We walk to the car. Grandma comes out to the car too. I feel the hitch in my throat as I look into her eyes. They are welling up with tears. She knows this goodbye is not the same as others. This is a long goodbye. Calgary is such a long way from home. Gone will be the weekend visits home. Gone will be the Christmas visits and birthday parties. She opens her arms to hug me. And I wrap my arms around her in tears.

"I love you, Mom," I choke out between the tight space in my throat.

I pull back and turn to Grandpa. His face is stricken even though he is smiling. There are silent tears forming in the corners of his eyes and flowing down his cheeks. I have only seen Grandpa cry one other time in my life, at his mom's funeral. This is more than I can take. I can see that he wants this to be different. I can see that he would beg us to stay if he could. He is losing his time with you. He knows that when we pull out of that driveway, his visits with you will never be the same. You will grow distant. You will grow up. You will grow apart.

He pulls you into his arms. He hugs you and cries on you.

"I love you, little buddy," he says.

I can't stop the floodgates now. I am sobbing. Dad makes motions for all of us to get into the car, as he knows this is not helpful. We are prolonging the pain of separation. The doors of the car slam shut. We roll down our windows for some last goodbyes and waves as we drive away from the camp.

We are all crying now. Our hearts are broken. We are choosing financial betterment over relationships. We are driving away from one path in life and choosing another. I don't know if we are right to do it. When we do go home for a visit, will we catch glimpses of what our lives could have been had we stayed?

There are two parallel universes stretching here before us. We are picking between them. I see the Christmases and celebrations we will miss, and the milestones we will pass over. I see the hugs and intimate things that will never be shared because of distance. There in the fabric alongside the memories we will make are those same memories in the parallel universe, but they are filled with family. In my heart I am making the choice that includes family, but that is not how life is playing out. There can be only one reality, and we are choosing to live it away from our families.

A few weeks later when I pick up the phone and call Grandpa and Grandma, the distance is obvious. The change I feared has come

102

true and a phone call is not enough. I listen to Grandpa tell me about cutting trees on our property or going hunting or fishing. Grandma tells me about volunteering or a bit about my brother and his family. I want to get to the real stuff, but there isn't time to build the safe circle around us on the phone. Intimacy is lost. They cannot tell me how they are really doing, and I cannot tell them either. It has to be enough but it isn't what relationships are built on. Relationships are formed from shared experiences and from reflection on things going on in our hearts. We can't get there on the phone.

You think there is time. But every week that passes are moments ticking off the finite clock of our time together, and I want to greedily grab memories before they are gone. You think years go by slowly, but time goes by without you noticing. One day I will turn around and my parents will be aged. There is no way to turn back so I can fill the photo album with vibrant pictures of the milestones I wished we'd had together. Instead, I will stare across the table at their feeble bodies with all the unshared memories as dust between us.

I wish we could have more years surrounded by people we love. This is a hard choice and one I might regret.

The Blue Funk

Me, looking back.

I was the crazy teenage girl crying herself to sleep every night, wanting to die, and worrying my parents sick that I would do something drastic while they sat there helpless, unable to make me less depressed. I outgrew the wanting to die feelings, but I'm not sure I have ever outgrown the blue funk. It resides in the in-between places. Whenever life is not going along well or if I am not busy enough, like a rank odour it starts to waft into my consciousness. It seems like if I just keep running fast enough, its smell won't reach my nose. The blue funk is simply a sense that life isn't worth the effort. It is not suicidal, because that would require some sort of effort. It is more like a resignation to the meaninglessness of it all and a lack of joy.

It is so easy to get prescriptions for this. I walked into my doctor's office a few years ago, broke into tears, and with the whisk of a pen and the rip of a notepad, I held a prescription for happy pills. I didn't take them. I am not advocating that people stop taking medication for depression, I am just saying how easy it is to get prescriptions for it. I can't talk about this freely because there is a stigma attached to mental illness and to not being able to cope. I must be deficient somehow to not happily thrive in our society. But how many of us need to be medicated before we realize that this needs to be addressed in a different way? If we aren't talking about it, we won't find a solution anytime soon.

I know that the happiness the media feeds us is empty and unfulfilling, but I haven't been able to replace it with something else. How can I? I don't have time to figure out what that looks like. I am too busy bustling around trying to achieve, purchase, acquire, accomplish, and strive. There is no time to reflect on where real joy and contentment come from. When I go on vacation, I catch glimpses of it. I often cry on my last day of vacation because I know I am shutting the door on my real life for a long time. I cry as I say goodbye to myself for another six months, until the next two-week visit.

It is uncomfortable to share this even with you. I want to appear strong and fulfilled. I want to say I've found the secrets to coping with this world. I want you to see me as someone in control. My emotions are too much a part of me, and I cannot adequately swallow them. They seep out of the seams in my clothes.

Business would be easier too if I didn't have such big emotions. People can read my face. I feel too much to have only transactional relationships. I have tried the stoic suit of armour and it chafed. It wore holes on my heart. Not all of me can show up at work. Putting too much of myself aside feeds my blue funk. It has been my biggest challenge in life to not allow my moods and emotions to be too overblown. I'm not sure if being successful at feeling less would be right, but it might have been easier.

Traditions

Cody, age 11. Me, age 34.

"Hey Mom, I need some pictures of myself to create a timeline of my life," you huff.

"Okay. Let's go look at the albums in the basement," I say, getting up and starting down the stairs. You follow reluctantly. I can tell you really want me to do this for you, but it is not my grade six project. There are about ten albums on the shelf.

I pull one down and hand it to you and then get one for myself. I open mine and smile at your wide, innocent, toothless grin. Your chin is wet with drool and your eyes are so blue. I can't believe how much you have grown since then and how fast it went. I pull out a picture of your first birthday and hand it to you. You find a picture of your first steps. I flip to the back of the album and see that it is all baby pictures. The next album is filled with pictures of you at age two. You open a different one and find pictures of you on top of a giant snowman. You are about five.

We flip through the rest.

"There aren't any pictures here for anything after I'm seven," you say angrily.

My stomach clenches as I realize this is true. My cheeks flush. I meant to take pictures, but Grandma and Grandpa always did that. We never carried our camera with us because they always did. When we moved away from them, we never learned to be the photographers. We moved away from photographic records of our lives.

"I'm sorry, Cody" I say embarrassed. "I guess we just aren't good at taking pictures."

I swallow hard at the realization that we don't have a way to step back in time and reminisce together over some photo albums. I should have captured your life. Why didn't I capture it?

You change so quickly from angry to carefree. You laugh and say, "Oh well, who needs more pictures of bad Halloween costumes and Thanksgiving turkeys."

I smile back, but inside a hot poker passes through my chest. I have failed you there too. The pictures aren't the only things missing. We no longer celebrate those holidays like we used to either.

Anniversaries and birthdays pass with little hoopla. We don't send cards, we don't bake cakes, and often we don't even buy gifts. Our family sucks at traditions and we have all sorts of excuses for it: cards are a waste of paper, holidays are too commercialized, and we should express our love all year not just on particular days. The truth is harder to admit. The truth is it takes effort to celebrate and I can't find the energy to do it for only the three of us.

I see the other moms baking things for the whole class. I see the other families posting family Christmas portraits. I see the other birthday parties you attend with decorations, invitations, games, and cake. I get tired looking at it all. I hold on to these excuses and you have even chimed in as we mock the card buying for meaningless holidays like Valentine's Day. You don't know any different, but I do.

I grew up with it all. Grandma sent the cards. Grandma baked the cakes, planned the games, and invited the kids. Grandma and Grandpa took the photos and built the photo albums. They made sure we had our fair share of large family Christmases and turkey with all the trimmings on Thanksgiving. They kept track of anniversaries and marked the milestones with a trip or a gift. They understood traditions and found the energy to make them happen. These traditions created a rhythm of time passing.

I look at the end of the photo albums. We cannot pull together a timeline of your life in photos because they weren't taken. You will not be able to share family holiday traditions with your future spouse because we don't really have any. You are missing the parts of life worth reminiscing over, the memories shared with opportunities for love to flow freely. We are skipping over those things to save energy and make things easier somehow. In the process we may be robbing you of some of the sweetest things in life. Not just cakes and cookies, but memories of warm family times and ties to who you are and where you come from. I regret this.

Parties

Cody, age 21. Me, age 44.

I walk into the ballroom and give the reception staff member my ticket. She smiles and hands me a fancy cocktail in a tall, slender glass. My eyes adjust to the dimly lit room but it is not dull. Red lights shine up the pillars of the room, festive music fills the space, and people are laughing and talking together in milling groups. A spinning clockwork of bodies like gears coming together exchanging energy and spinning once more. I grab Dad's hand and we make our way into the room to find our friends.

I spot a few of them at a table in the centre of the room and we walk to join them. Everyone looks relaxed and people are leaning in to talk to each other over the din of the room. I hug a few of my friends and introduce Dad to those who have not met him yet. Our table has tall bar stools and I climb up onto one near the middle of the table to be able to talk to the most people. Dad pulls up one beside me and puts his arm on my waist briefly as he gets comfortable. My cocktail is producing a warm glow in my cheeks already as I haven't eaten since lunch.

I ask one friend about her latest online-engagement project. "It is so much more fun this year. I have changed things up and people are really loving it," she responds. I turn to a friend's spouse and ask him, "How were your Christmas holidays? Did your girls both make it home?" The conversation bubbles up like champagne, a tickling, sparkling effervescence. We are knitting our connections together here across the table of drinks and food. The pleasantries are shifting now to deeper conversations about family and life, dreams for the future, and the rough spots of this year. My heart opens as I feel the kinship here.

The live band comes on. I can feel the music in my chest, a rumble of bass and drums. My ears ring slightly as the higher notes of the guitar and woman's voice are amplified through the space. I turn to Dad and try to yell into his ear. He leans in hard to hear me but there is no way for him to catch my words as the music pushes my voice around. I take another deep breath and try again and Dad smiles and nods. I know he can't hear me because the nod is dismissive and his smile is sympathetic but disconnected. I watch as the ties between all of us shrivel into ephemeral threads as we focus on our drinks and try to look engaged with attempts to bop along to the music.

It is lonely now at this party. It doesn't seem right. How can I be in a space filled with festivities and friends and yet feel so alone with myself? I see the shadows of some of the dancers on the wall and how they look like stretched-out caricatures. I want to point this out to someone but my words are lost in the clamour. I am alone with my thoughts and observations even though I am right here sharing this experience with everyone else. They too are in solitude, witnessing it but unable to commune.

This party is amplifying the gap between myself and others. Even here in full celebration of life, we are never really together. This truth stings. I don't want to know this reality. I work hard to create a feeling of connection with others through shared space, shared laughter, and shared thoughts. Try as I might to break through the separation, I cannot bridge that chasm. I can only send notes and flares across its expanse. And this is the sadness inside a party.

Sorry

Cody, age 12. Me, age 35.

Dad and I come home from volunteering with a green non-profit organization. We are doing in-home audits and helping people switch to better light bulbs, low-flow shower heads, and safer cleaning products. I am jazzed up and feeling electric.

"I think she really got it!" I say to Dad, thinking about how excited this woman was about how much power and water she could save.

"I don't know," Dad groans. "Even if she makes all the changes, the size of that house can only be so efficient."

I see his point. The vibrancy in my veins drains out and a heaviness comes over me. I have felt this before when my idealistic viewpoint comes up against reality. It is only one house with a meagre environmental footprint compared with industry. Our households can be as efficient as possible, and we still won't make a big enough shift to match the usage of industry, or the destruction elsewhere in the world either. My forehead wrinkles at the concern I have for our planet combined with the magnitude of the shift to be made.

When I graduated from university I was sure my generation would make a difference. We would know more than our parents and make better choices. We would show them. I really thought it could be different. I truly believed that with just the right pressure, with the right sales pitch, heck, with just doing what is "right," that things could change. I was still optimistic and naive when I brought you into this world. I mothered you dreaming of a world of possibility for you. I imagined you being able to make your way in this world with ease and seeing how our generation turned things around.

113

It just isn't to be. I think about you up in your room unaware of the loss before you. You will see the climate change. You won't know songbirds like I've known songbirds. I can't protect you. My money won't sway politicians and create policy. My voice is too timid in this city where oil is the livelihood of so many. I still drive my car, buy bleached toilet paper, and fly on a plane for vacations.

I'm sorry. I'm sorry for the world you have been brought into. I am sorry I cannot protect you from the pain and suffering that it will bring. I am sorry my generation and the generation before me failed you.

You interrupt my thoughts and say, "Come listen to my new guitar riff." I go up to your room and stand in the doorway while you get your guitar onto your lap. You look down at the strings and tentatively strum out a famous guitar lick. It is slow and choppy, but you are so proud. You look up at me innocent and hopeful. You are not thinking about the future. You are ready for the world and whatever comes your way. You have hope and optimism.

I lean against the doorframe as you play another, more practiced guitar piece. I see the world as things we've lost and you don't know it any other way. I have heard the battle cry against climate change and also seen the tipping point of no return. I have witnessed massive exploitation, extinction, and degeneration, but my memory also carries the world that was before that. You only know the earth as a scarred place, so you do not grieve its loss in the same way. I am sorry our world is broken, even if you don't know it now. I worry you will ask me why we didn't do more to stop it. I only hope that your optimism will carry you along and that you forgive me for what I could have done. You continue to play your guitar, focusing on the here and now and washing away worry with your music. I wish my worry could wash away so easily.

SECTION 5: CHEERS

Gratitude

Cody, age 21. Me, age 44.

Today is just an ordinary day like any other ordinary day. I am sitting here in the early morning light drinking my coffee. But wait, I think, I am sitting here in a body that can bend and touch and move! I am not only drinking this comforting liquid, I can feel it warming my insides! How incredible it is now that I notice Dad. I am but centimetres away from another living being who is breathing and communing with me, whose heart is beating like mine, who is thinking their thoughts and feeling their feelings right there beside me! I see the glow of the early morning light. The sun is rising in the sky! The day is breaking! How magnificent to have eyes! How astonishing it is to be alive! I want to tell everyone about the miracle of life but there just aren't any words.

This sensation is too powerful to share with anyone. It is beyond expression and would lose its strength in trying to speak it out loud. It feels like a train barreling through my chest and it sends rhythmic vibrations through my veins. It is a swelling up of emotion so powerful that it brings tears to my eyes. I feel as though I need to run around and tell people how I am feeling, share some amazing secret, or burst into dance or song. It is simply gratitude, but on a level that is all-encompassing. This doesn't happen to me often, I wish it did, but it is so memorable that I know long after it has stopped it will still be close enough to feel. Why did it come to me now while I am drinking a coffee like I have countless other mornings? Can I make it come again? It is this gratitude that I need in my mundane life. This is what makes my average life special, my journey extraordinary, and my life more abundant.

I have spent some of my years chasing things. More money, a better title, a bigger house, a life in a city, and when I achieved all those things, I realized there were still other things I didn't have. There will always be other things. Even if I were one of the richest people in the world, there would still be things I didn't possess and things I still wanted. I am not fully practiced at this, but I am now focusing more on the things I do have, the experiences I have gone through, and the abundance that does surround me.

It is arrogant of me to think I am lacking. I probably have more than the six billion other people on the planet do, just because I was born in Canada. But gratitude can be tough to cultivate. Our culture sends us messages every day that we are still lacking in something. I could be more beautiful, have more luxury, and travel to more places. There is no TV channel playing all the things I *do* have. This is the channel I need to grow in my own mind; build a reel of the gifts that I already possess. My reel would include a loving husband, a family that instilled a strong work ethic in me, friends that are available anytime I need them, a safe country, a house to live in, abundant food, and sufficient money.

My average life is really not so average when I list all of these things. There is a richness in the recognition of my blessings, I just don't always see it. I spend many days planning my business, working through to-do lists, and imagining the future. Each of these activities is a focus on what is yet to be done, experienced, and taken care of. I don't dedicate enough time to things I have accomplished, milestones I have experienced, and gifts I have been given.

I want to stay here in this moment with the rush of emotion. I want to remember this and conjure it up again and again and share what I can of it with my loved ones. Gratitude is a powerful force and changes how I see everything.

I Enjoy Music in a Way That Is Almost Obscene

Cody, age 21. Me, age 44.

I can hear your music through the closed bathroom door. You have your shower speaker cranked and let your music blast out for all of us to enjoy. I smile as I hear my music, slightly muffled but undeniable, coming from your shower. This was not always the case. I can remember hearing the bass pounding through the floor from your room and worrying that the neighbours would complain. Screaming guitar, screaming voices, and dark lyrics are not something I enjoyed then or now.

You finish up your shower and get dressed. I am sitting in my office and you stop in the doorway with your phone. "Hey Mom, I heard this song the other day, you might like it." You hit play and I listen to it. It fits into my repertoire. It is acoustic and warm. It has no screaming guitar or metal lyrics. I smile. "Thanks. And who was the artist again?" I ask. Such a funny change from a few short years ago. I remember when you would come downstairs and open the fridge. Standing there gazing into the shelves for a snack, you would overhear my music playing. You mocked the lyrics as you sung along to Jack Johnson. You rejected my music to create a difference between us. And now here you are sharing your music with me. Now it is something we will both like. You are mirroring me and we are coming together again.

There is something fabulous about music. I do not play an instrument, nor can I sing, but I enjoy music in a way that is almost obscene. I am sure many other people feel this way too. Music has the power to transport me away from my reality to a time in the past with vivid memory recall or to a time in the future with luscious dreams. It can be delicious and intoxicating. The music I choose to listen to makes me feel connected, whole, and warm. I wonder if you are listening to my music because it makes you feel that way too?

119

There is something else fascinating about music. The pictures and colours and brain tickles it brings me. It is no wonder that people have been making music for centuries and are drawn in by music. People with mental disabilities, the elderly, those who are non-verbal all exhibit pleasure when listening to music. It does something to the soul at the same time as to the ear. And yet so often we take it for granted. I do not necessarily think about integrating it into my day for particular effects. Yet, how powerful would that be to intentionally structure my music to correspond to what I need at every moment? (I think there is an app for that!)

The music I love most has a lot of emotion tied to it. Either it can help me recall memories or feelings from the past (the music of my childhood) or it can tug immediately at my heartstrings. It is this emotional tie that makes music special to me. The memories I have when listening to music are not necessarily detailed—very often they are merely feelings, and often simply feelings of nostalgia. I can "feel" the simpler times in my life when listening to seventies music. "The Age of Aquarius" or anything by the Carpenters instantly transports me to the pig-tailed girl living in a small town.

Corey Hart, Prince, and U2 can make me instantly feel the raw self-awareness and angst of my teen years. The Barenaked Ladies and the Tragically Hip make me feel lost and lonely like I was in university. There are other periods in my life that have a few musical ties. "Life Is a Highway" by Tom Cochrane transports me to road trips with Dad, "Lady in Red" brings up an old boyfriend, and "Holiday" by Green Day is a snapshot of your first concert, just you and me.

And now I will have this song to remind me of our mutual love of warm friendly music, right here in my office after your shower.

Letting Go of Money

Me, looking back.

Dad and I lost more money in 2008 than I care to think about. We lost your RESP. We lost our retirement funds. We lost much of our security. It hurt so much, even more so because we were trading it ourselves. We couldn't blame someone else. We didn't have enough knowledge to see the crash coming. We were so naive. Dad and I fought about it, blamed each other, and grieved. We had to replace our dreams of retirement with something new. We questioned what money meant to us. It was hard.

There is no denying that I have had a complex relationship with money. I need it to survive in this world and at the same time it is no guarantee of my survival. It establishes the haves and the have-nots but does little to ensure me a rich life. It defines status and yet says nothing about my character. My relationship to its complexity will take a lifetime to sort through, and I'm still sorting.

Money has a lot of emotional charge for me because it is still the most tangible representation of my self-worth. I know this is ridiculous, but on the one hand, I see it as a sign of security, a representation of success, and a tie to the dreams I have for me and my family. On the other hand, I also know it cannot measure my relationships, my humanity, or my love. I give it too much power, though. It is a painful reminder of financial decisions that didn't go well and opportunities and paths not taken. This is part of the work I have left to do in unravelling my relationship to it.

I believe that money is flow. The more each of us grasps and tries to hold on to it, the less money there is "in play," the slower the trickle or flow. The more money each of us spends freely, the more money there is making the world go round. A gush of abundance. We all play a part in this flow, no matter how much money we have.

Now, don't get me wrong, this is not an argument for thoughtless consumer behaviour. Spending money on trivial items does not align with my beliefs. There are ramifications for mindless purchasing. What we need is flow, not the disregard of our future or the environment. So this flow must include our values: thoughtful spending. And thoughtful spending includes money shared with others or donated to charities and non-profits. Money needs to move, but it needs to do so with integrity.

I will not get into the deep discussion about the economics behind money and flow. There are plenty of books about that. I want to share my own relationship to this flow and why sometimes I can pour it out like water and other times I bottle it up as fast as I can.

From what I have learned about myself and money, it all comes down to my perception of the future. When I feel certain that the future will provide, I can release money easily. When I feel uncertain about the future, I save like a miser. You are a saver. Is it because you feel insecure about the future? If we are all feeling uncertain, money doesn't move. Scarcity becomes a self-fulfilling prophecy as we are all busy saving. We reduce the money in flow and there is less to go around.

To release it even in times of uncertainty, I need faith. Faith in our family's ability to make enough money to cover our needs. Faith in being creative, adaptive, and wise no matter what the world serves up. This faith has been fuelled by the deliberate storing up of memories of our past ability to overcome. Recalling these memories is usually enough, but there seems to be more to it than just faith.

Beyond faith, I need to replace money's powerful representations with something else. Money represents a few things for me: security, success, and the ability to achieve our dreams. I need to replace these with something else. If my security is not in my money, where will it come from? If my success is not represented by my money, what form does my achievement take? If my dreams are constrained by money, how can I dream dreams that can be fulfilled no matter my financial state? Finding these substitutions is something only I can do for me and you can do for you.

As I find my faith in the future and as I paint a strong picture of success and dreams beyond money, I get closer to being able to release money with more ease. But the work doesn't stop there either. The decision to release it comes with the responsibility of releasing it with integrity and intention. What this means shifts for me at different times. Sometimes I am called to share, sometimes I am called to invest in an opportunity such as my own education, and sometimes I am called to make a purchase to add to our daily living.

It is the thoughtful examination of the release of money that sends it out into the world with power and intention. How did I choose to share it? Will the recipient be a steward of the money, and will they create impact? What opportunity did I invest in, and how will I use this investment for our betterment? What item did I purchase? Was it made sustainably, and will it add ease to our lives? When my money is released into the world with great intention behind it, it flows from me more easily.

I want to share my awareness of the complexity of my relationship to money with you to save you some time. I know that my ability to let it go is reliant on my certainty in the future and my faith in our ability to adapt, my ability to define success, security, and dreams beyond money, and my careful examination of my intentions when I choose to release it. I am learning to master its release and let it flow so that I can give it wings to not only bless me but bless others.

Kindness

Cody, age 21. Me, age 44.

I have just started to ride the bus. I take it two days a week to work downtown with a client. I look up my bus stop on the transit website and trudge through the snow to the glassed-in shelter near our house. Two parka-clad people greet me at the bus stop.

"I am new to this again. It's been eight years since I rode the bus into downtown," I share with them. "I just hope I get off at the right stop."

"I am sure you will," one lady chimes in.

I am too nervous to look around at anyone on the bus. I am focusing on figuring out when to get off. I don't want to make a mistake and have to walk far in the bitter morning cold. My stop comes up on the digital display in the bus and I get off at the right place. Now to get home with the same ease.

I walk up to the bus stop the next morning more relaxed.

"How are you today?" I ask.

"Good," the parka-clad lady responds. "Did you get off the bus okay yesterday?"

"I did, thanks," I say back, chuckling.

I feel comfortable here and know that it won't be long before we know each other well. They are only five-minute conversations while we wait for the bus, but I know we will use them to build familiarity. Today I can look around at my fellow passengers. I feel the strangest connection to them. All of them. We are neighbours. We live in close enough proximity that we get on the same bus. We are all heading to our work for the day, early in the morning, bleary eyed and bundled up against the cold. We have all left our warm homes and families behind and are heading out into the world to make some money and contribute to society.

I imagine that I could lean over to any one of them to talk and they would talk back comfortably. I also imagine that if, God forbid, our bus were to encounter trouble, we would band together and take care of each other. I have never thought about that before. So often I have looked out at a sea of strangers and simply thought of them as a crowd— no connection, no humanity, just obstacles in my way. What if instead I always thought of them as my neighbours, or people who would return a favour if I extended one to them? It would be a different world. And as they get off the bus, in my head I wish them well for the day.

I am sitting with a middle-aged woman today. We are both busy with our phones reading as we make our way into the downtown core. As the stops begin, we both pack up our things. I notice that she has blue bus tickets in her hand. The blue tickets are not the current fare price, and I have a few back home as well. It's odd she is holding them in her hand as she is getting off. Don't they have transfers if she is getting on another bus?

I lean over and ask, "I see you have some blue tickets. Do you just add some change and when you use them?"

She replies, "There is a grace period where they accept them as full fare."

"Oh good! I have some at home." I say and smile.

After a stop or two more, the seat in front of us opens up so I shift there to make it easier for her to get off, as my stop is one of the last. She gets up too and sits with a woman in the seat in front of me. She greets the woman warmly, and passes her the book of bus tickets. The exchange is simple, the price of the tickets fairly nominal but the gratitude the receiving woman expresses tells me that it is no small gift.

She needs those bus tickets, they will make a difference to her life, and I see a wide smile on her face but I also notice her shoulders relax and a warmth spreads between them that even I can feel.

How many things like this happen every day?

Are we paying attention, do we notice the kindnesses when they occur?

Are we the ones bringing them into being?

I hope so.

SECTION 6: BEST WISHES

There Is No Perfect Path

Cody, not yet born. Me, 20–21 and looking back.

I am the good girl. I get good grades. I don't smoke, drink, or do drugs. And still, it is not enough.

I want to move in with Dad in my second year of university, and I can hear my parents' disapproval over the phone line.

"It will be cheaper than getting my own place," I explain.

"Yeah, but you aren't married," they argue back.

"I'm old enough to know what I am doing. I won't get pregnant," I say. I can't make them too angry—they are still helping to pay for my schooling and I need their help. They relent. How could they stop me when I am miles away anyway?

It is tough. Dad and I struggle with who will do the dishes and clean the bathroom. We don't have much money and sleep on a mattress without a frame or box spring. The apartment we rent is in the basement of a house and the landlord turns our heat off and comes into our apartment when we aren't home. It isn't ideal but we struggle along.

I begin to think about what else could make me happier. Maybe if we got married that would make me happy? I bring the subject up to Dad. He laughs at first and then sees how serious I am. He proposes a few weeks later.

"Mom, Dad, I have some news," I fret on the phone that weekend.

"Oh?" Mom worries.

"Schaene and I are engaged!" I blurt. There is silence on the other end of the phone.

"You are what?" Dad asks.

"Engaged," I repeat.

"We can't afford a wedding," Mom remarks.

"I know. We want to keep it small and find ways to keep the expenses down," I babble. I decide not to tell them that I have already bought my dress from a garage sale we went to last week. I can't seem to win. I can't live in sin and I can't get married either. The wedding plans go ahead and all of the plans are made over the Christmas holidays and over the phone for a May 1 wedding. Dad and I get married at 21 years old.

My parents were probably right. I was too young to be getting married. We were going to have a tough go of it as we still had so much growing up to do, but you couldn't have told me that then. I was still in the invincible youth years and sure we could conquer anything.

We have, but it has been hard. I didn't live out the perfectly prescribed path of everyone's dreams. Maybe it would have been easier and maybe it wouldn't have. But what I do know is there is no perfect path. There will be twists and turns for all of us. You will have to make your choices despite what the world tells you, but you will have to live with the consequences of those choices too. Dad and I grew up so rapidly together. We conquered financial difficulty, finding ourselves, and building a life and family out of nothing. We have those triumphs to look back on as things we would not have done if we had not gotten married so young. Don't fret if you take a path less chosen; it might just be the path that leads to the best things for you.

The Loss of Unrealized Expectation

Cody, not yet born. Me age, 16.

I stand in front of the mirror and check my hair. My bangs are backcombed and my long, permed hair frames my face in three inches of curls and hairspray. I dig through my closet for the right shirt to go with my tight jeans. Something hip enough to say "I might," but conservative enough to say "but not tonight." I throw on a little dark eyeliner to finish the look.

I live 20 minutes from the high school, and luckily our school arranges the same buses as they do for regular classes. I get on the bus and sit in the front half with a friend. I let my mind wander to the possibility of meeting someone. I imagine his hands on my back and the smell of his cologne as we slow dance. I worry his hands will run over my muffin top above my jeans or he will see the new pimple on my chin. Maybe tonight there will be the right guy who can look past all that and we will dance and dance and maybe even kiss as we say goodbye.

The school cafeteria is dark and the music vibrates against the walls. It is the same crowd with the same cliques forming here and there. The jocks and the pretty girls, the smokers, who appear to have been drinking already, and the rest of us who don't really fit in, holding up the walls, leaning against our hands, and trying to look cooler than we feel. The dance floor fills and empties with the rise and fall of the music. Groups of girls dance together as a poor replacement for having a dance partner. I try to smile with my friends, but I also scan the dark edges of the room, hoping to find the boy of my daydream.

Two hours later, "Stairway to Heaven" comes on. It's the final song of every dance. A long, close cuddle for those who have a partner, an excruciatingly long reminder to the rest of us that we are alone. Most of the single people don't wait to see it through. We head for the buses and the safety of their dark seats. No boy swept me off my feet. No romcom sappy happy ending. The bus smells like old musty socks and matches the revulsion I feel about myself. I lean my forehead against the cold, single-paned window and pretend I am looking out into the starry night. I hope no one notices the tears that roll down my cheeks. Why did I think tonight would be any different? Why did I get my hopes up? I had admonished myself for my daydreams and how naive I was. I am not to be the teenage boy's fantasy. When will I learn not to lean in to the anticipation? My expectations only lead to disappointment. Would I have had more fun with my friends if I had gone with only them in my mind?

I stretch and pretend to yawn and then I rub my eyes as though I am tired, but I use that gesture to wipe my tears away. I will not do this again if I can help it. I will let life come, but I will not conjure up expectations only to have them dashed by reality. It is too painful. Instead I will see what story is really being told and enjoy that. Instead of a pile of broken dreams, I will have a mountain of unexpected experiences and try to find my joy in that.

You Only Get One Go

Cody, age 9. Me, age 32.

I can see them on the horizon, the grey-and-white peaks of the Rocky Mountains. They just seem to appear out of nowhere across the flat prairie, and I can't help but inhale when confronted by their magnificence. I have seen them before when I was 16, but that was so long ago. I point them out to you and you lean forward in your van seat to get a better view. Dad smiles. He has only ever flown over them and this will be his first trip driving through them. Dad and I are heading to a friend's wedding in British Columbia, and we are making it a vacation at the same time.

We watch the mountains slowly get bigger and bigger as we drive closer. It is amazing how far away you can be and still see them. I look over at you and watch your excitement as we finally drive into them. You can't get enough and are craning your neck to look up past the roof of the van to see the tops of the mountains beside us. They tower over each side of the road, and their peaks are often hidden beyond the clouds. They have such presence; I feel protected and exhilarated at the same time. There is nothing like this in Ontario, despite all the rugged natural spaces there. The mountains are different somehow.

The wedding is on the Labour Day weekend, the last long weekend before school starts in September. I get up early and help erect a wildflower-covered arch in the backyard for the ceremony. The mountains surround us on all sides and nestle us in their protective shoulders. I feel drawn to this spot, this landscape, and the adventurous spirit in me is kindled. The wedding guests are rugged and casual. They are rock climbers, mountain bikers, hikers, and musicians. There is a palpable connectedness between the people and the land here. I want this.

We get up early the next morning. We have no time to waste and will be attempting to drive the entire way back to Ontario without stopping. It is about 36 hours of driving, but school starts on Tuesday and Dad needs to get back to work too. I can't shake my sense of loss and dread as the mountains become tinier and tinier in the rearview mirror. I have never felt so connected to a place before and my mind starts playing with possibilities. Could we move here? What would we do for a living? Where would we live?

I check to see if you are sleeping. You are slumped over in your seat, trying to catch up after staying up for all the wedding night festivities.

"What do you think of the mountains?" I ask Dad.

"They are beautiful. Why?" he says, sensing there is more to my question.

"Could we move here?" I timidly ask, afraid of what he might say.

"I don't know. What are you thinking?" he pries.

"I think Calgary has the closest stores I could transfer to. Should I try?" I ask, hopeful.

"Okay," he says, but I sense he is hoping nothing comes of this. He has already given up so much for me. He closed the doors on our first business to make our first move for my first promotion, and he is feeling settled into his job in North Bay, but I am ready for something else after three years.

I scour the internal job boards as soon as I return to work. There is a posting for Calgary, and I bring it to my store manager and ask her opinion. She is supportive of this as my next move, and so I apply. It all happens so fast. Without time to reconsider, I am packing my bags to start work there after Thanksgiving weekend. Dad is staying behind in

136

North Bay for a few weeks to pack the house and get it ready to sell while I find us a new house in Calgary.

We are leaping at life. Dad and I have developed a saying for these moments: "You only get one go, so you might as well go." Life is not long, and it is not for sitting on the sidelines in fear. This move is full of uncertainty but that's also what makes it exciting. This move is full of possible regrets but equally it is full of possible triumphs. We will go. We will try together and we will make the most of this adventure together.

Reward the Shifters

Me, looking back.

I still haven't mastered how to best use my gifts and talents in this world. Maybe there will never be a lightning-bolt clear focus, and maybe I will not be able to put my finger directly on the "thing." But what I do know is that with the amount of uncertainty happening in our world, all I can really hope for is to be able to shift and use my gifts in whatever situation I find myself in. And you, too.

It is almost laughable when someone asks me, "What do you want to be doing in five years?" Not because I don't want to dream or to have goals, but because I cannot know what the world will look like in that amount of time. What will have happened in the economy? What will the political climate be? What environmental catastrophes will have happened? I cannot know now what the world will be. I can only rest in the knowledge that no matter where I find myself, I can shift and draw on my gifts and talents to get through.

I graduated from university in 1994 and moved with Dad from Guelph back to the Sault area. I had worked my summers of university with the Ministry of Environment, Forestry Canada, and various professors, building up the network and experience I needed to land my first job. And then I didn't. There was a hiring freeze in the government, and biology jobs just weren't that plentiful in the north. But we made do. We looked around for other opportunities and transitioned our skills and talents to other things. That was the first time I shifted and changed, and I haven't stopped doing that.

Some would peg me as a quitter, or at least someone who is highly unstable. I have had seven careers: biologist, window installer, retail manager, event planner, professional organizer, kitchen installer, and business consultant. Crazy. Maybe I have left some financial growth on the table as I made these switches, but I didn't leave my soul behind. Every job change I made was for something better: a more interesting position, a more supportive culture, or a more desirable lifestyle. What I learned through all those changes was my ability to shift, learn, adapt, and succeed.

That is why it is so important to develop an ability to embrace uncertainty and change. I believe the world needs flexible, strategic, and brave people. We need self-starters, fearless experimenters, and opportunity seizers. We need optimists, community builders, and connectors. We need problem-solvers and visionaries. Above all, we need people who include people and the environment in all their thinking. I want you never to be afraid of being one of these people.

It is time to reward the shifters. It is time to embrace our inner butterfly and flit and flap from thing to thing. Enough with the past. Enough with stagnation and long-term employment. We are the future, and the future is erratic.

Thank Your Influences

Cody, age 13. Me, age 36.

I am so excited. We just purchased 100 acres of land back home, and Dad and I are talking about moving there instead of living here in Calgary. We have always wanted a farm and want to live off the land. One hundred acres should be enough, and we will be close to family too. The land is only a few kilometres from where Dad grew up. You will be able to have some of the same experiences as he did: dirt biking the bush trails, cutting firewood, helping out with the garden and animals. I think about who our neighbours might be and who you might be able to make friends with. There aren't many houses out there. Kilometres stretch between the mailboxes that dot the road—little posts letting you know that behind the trees, someone lives in that spot.

I feel the nostalgia rising as I think about one of my high school teachers who lives out there. She probably doesn't know the difference she made in my life. I struggled with dark thoughts in high school and had a hard time dreaming about what I could become. She used her biology class to connect with me. She talked about women in science. She painted a picture of possibility and success for me. She lifted me up and gave me some dreams far beyond what I had been shooting for. She probably doesn't even know how grateful I am and that I wouldn't have finished my science degree without her voice in my mind encouraging me.

I hear the small voice in my head say, "Let her know." I am sentimental that way. I still wear my heart on my sleeve and boldly say the vulnerable things most of us think but never utter out loud. I should have no trouble sending a note. Her address will be easy because it is a rural route, and all I need is her name and the postal code my husband grew up with. A card will get to her without fail. I rummage in my stationery drawer and find a blank card. I pour out a message of thanks to her for her influence on me and how that affected my life. I find a stamp, seal the envelope, and pop it in the mail.

I think about my own influence on others. I am a Scout leader, and I watched Grandpa while I was growing up work so hard as a teacher to help his students. Like him, I care so deeply about the kids in my troop. Each year the kids' faces come and go. Sometimes I have those moments when I hope I make a difference in their lives. I don't want my teacher to wonder if she had any impact beyond the curriculum she taught; I want her to *know*. She made a difference in my life and I want to tell her. I also think about the other people I would call mentors. I have had women who demonstrated their strength and leadership in our community, women who voluntarily shared their gifts and talents with me, and people who saw me in all my messy immaturity and helped to send me on my way. I am blessed.

I pick up the mail a few weeks later. I can see the square envelope standing tall among the bills and statements. Our address is handwritten on the front with my name in flowing script above it. I walk home from the mailbox savouring the anticipation of opening it. I toss the rest of the mail onto the kitchen table and bring the letter to my living room chair. I pull my legs up and cozy in as my heart swells and I begin to read. She is grateful and overwhelmed. She had always wondered if she had made a difference. She is happy to know and humbled too. I can picture her writing this note and I am transported back to biology class. She is leaning over my shoulder to show me how to dissect my frog and I feel her genuine concern for my success.

I am grateful for her and I am filled with gratitude for having the chance to tell her the difference she made to me. This is a vulnerable exchange, but there isn't any better kind.

Potential Is Not Enough

Cody, not yet born. Me, age 18.

"Another university letter has come," Grandma shouts down the hall at me.

I run into the kitchen and grab it. It's from the last university I have yet to hear back from. I am so nervous. I want this one so bad: systems design engineering. I start to open it and feel the blood surge to my chest. My fingers fumble and I crinkle the letter significantly as I pull it out of the half-opened envelope. I unfold the letter. Accepted.

"I got in!" I exclaim.

"Your Dad will be so proud," Grandma says.

I sigh with relief. Making Grandpa proud, doing something worth doing, and living up to my potential is all I have ever wanted to do. A second passes and reality sets in. How will I choose? I've been accepted to all the programs I applied to, and I am not sure how to choose between biomedical engineering and systems design engineering. I don't know what these programs even really mean, but my guidance counsellors and parents think they will match my abilities.

I decide to attend the systems design program. I fill out my acceptance form and walk to the post office a block from my house. I open the mail shoot and put the letter in. The spring loaded door slams shut and I feel compelled to open the door and stick my arm in. Wait! I've made a terrible mistake. I shouldn't take that program. I should take the biomedical one instead. I open the door and peer in. There is a metal scoop that prevents me from seeing the mail and reaching in. It is done. I cannot turn back.

The welcome package comes in the mail a few weeks later. It is crisp, formal, and congratulatory. This is a sought-after program and I should be honoured, but all I can think is that I have chosen wrong. I place the package on my desk beside the other acceptance letter and stare at the name of the other program's dean in its top corner. I grab it and walk to the living room. Grandma is sitting in her chair rocking gently and knitting. She looks up at me and can see that I need to talk.

"Mom," I start quietly and slowly. "I think I've made the wrong choice," I say.

"Oh?" Grandma says.

"I am excited to go to the university I accepted, but I keep thinking that this program might be better for me," I say and hold out the letter.

"What do you want to do?" she asks.

"I want to call and see if they still have space for me," I say.

"You need to decide," she says.

I pick up the phone and talk to the dean. He is gracious and understanding. He hears me struggling with this decision, but he says he would love to have me in his program. I hang up the phone and wait for the relief to come. It doesn't. I immediately think, "But wait! I've made the wrong choice again!"

I am only 18. I don't know what this decision will mean for me. How much of my future am I determining with this one decision? I want to do the right thing and "be all that I can be," but this potential is killing me. I essentially could be anything. But that means I could be anything! Is there someone who can help me narrow it down? And truthfully, can someone say it is okay that I don't really want either of these choices? Didn't my aptitude test say I should be a social worker?

I pick up the phone again a few weeks later. I am calling the first program's dean to see if he can take me back. He doesn't seem thrilled, but I explain how hard this choice is for me, that his school is prestigious, and that I would want my degree from there. He accepts me back in.

I arrive at the university wide-eyed and nervous. I am from rural Northern Ontario and there are more people in one of the dorms than in my entire town. With a lot of map reading and walking, I find my frosh-week group and get a schedule of all the activities. My group invites me to a barbecue just off campus and mentions it is BYOB. I am so torn. I don't know anyone here and it would sure be nice to fit in, but I am underage, parties aren't my scene, and I don't want to navigate my way home in the dark in a city I hardly know alone. I decide against the party and catch the next bus home. I will attend some of the scheduled events the next day.

I arrive on campus early the next morning and make my way to the engineering building. Frosh leaders, coloured ribbons, clipboards, and what looks like kiddie pools filled with mud are packed into the field in front of the building. I have a pretty good idea of how this is going to go. I paste on my best smile and summon some courage. I follow my team through the mud obstacles. As we slosh through the kiddie pools, we are sprayed with coloured dye from water-pistol-wielding frosh leaders. My ear is filled with mud. My face and shirt are now tie-dyed and my clothes, shoes, and skin are wet and muddy. We join a large crowd of baptized froshers and chant some allegiances to the school and this discipline. Among all these testosterone-fuelled engineer wannabes, all I feel is loneliness. My only thoughts are about how I'm going to ride a public transit bus across the city covered in dye and mud.

I attend only a few other events, just enough to say that I participated in frosh week. I still haven't met anyone from my program. There are so many different kinds of engineers here and my program is small. I haven't been attending the evening parties and I don't live on campus to meet people in the dorms. I am finding it hard to get to know people. Hopefully this morning I will meet some friends, because classes are starting today. I sit in the back of the lecture hall of my first class and look down at the heads in front of me. It is a sea of short male hair. I see only two other women in the 90 or so people in the room. I pick up my books and move to sit beside one of the other women. I smile at her and introduce myself.

The lecture hall quiets down as a few men stand at the front of the room. One begins talking about the program and what is to be expected. He asks us to look at the person beside us. I look at the woman I just met. She looks at me. He asks us which one of us will be here next year, because 50 percent of the people who start the program fail. I see her eyes steel. I feel my heart squeeze. This is not what I want. I don't want a rival, I want a friend. I need someone to hearten me in a program I don't feel cut out for. I don't want to be pitted against the only person I've met so far who might be my friend.

I want to make my parents proud, but I don't really want this. I want to do something with my life, but I am not prepared for this competitive, lonely environment. I am smart, but I am not willing to fight for something I never really wanted anyway. I walk out of the lecture hall numb and desperate for an escape. I can feel the dark thoughts rushing in. I don't want them to take hold. I need to find help and so I look for a campus phone. I leaf through the tattered phone book and find the number for the guidance office. The soonest appointment they have is in three days. I take it.

The next few days are a blur of classes and readiness exams. I fail a couple of those. I can feel my confidence slipping further. How did I end up here? Hopefully my guidance counsellor appointment will shed some light on what I can do. I walk into the guidance office and shake the counsellor's hand. I tell her my name and she nods and says, "And what is your student number?" I am only a number here. I don't want to be a number. I came to this office to find someone who could see me, who might be able to provide a warm, understanding suggestion of how I can get through this. I am only a number. I swallow hard and batten down the hatches. I am in this alone. I don't remember what we talked about except that when I left the office, I was transferring into the science program the next week.

It isn't my parents' fault. They only want what is best for me. They encourage me and give me wings. It isn't my teachers' fault. They only kindle the spark they see. It isn't the school's fault; it isn't its job to buoy up the spirits of an ill-prepared small town girl.

I am a young woman with wings and dreams, filled to the brim with potential. But potential is not enough to sustain me. What appears to be a gift of possibility, something of substance to hang on to, is instead insufficient, a facade.

My potential is a pair of rose-coloured glasses. Or is it a pair of blinders? I am left here alone with no direction. I make a final grasp at a science degree that might be prestigious enough, but I feel I am letting people down. It's a harsh reality when the promise of potential fails. My potential is but a balloon filled with air that can buoy my spirit, but it is not strong enough to lift me now. I wish I could go back and arrive here with something more substantial.

Toward Abundance

Cody, age 1–3. Me, age 24–26.

I hear the phone ringing again and know better than to answer it. It is probably someone trying to collect money from us. Dad is at work and I am home with you. You are finally sleeping and I hope the phone won't wake you. I fold another cloth diaper from the pile that I just finished washing. I am so thankful we have these diapers. I cannot imagine how we would have afforded disposables.

Dad will be home in a few hours and we will have to talk. Our rent is paid this month, but I don't think we can pay next month's if we are going to make all the other payments. Leaving university with a ten-year plan of student loan debt and no jobs (at least, no great-paying jobs) is not what I had envisioned. If you want to do the right thing in Canada and pay your debts off, there isn't a great system to do that. The welfare office told us to claim bankruptcy. I don't want to. Bankruptcy is a difficult road of trying to build your credit back up and we want to buy a house sooner rather than later. If we don't claim bankruptcy, our meagre monthly allotment will not pay our student loans and our rent and food. It is one or the other. Every month we are on welfare, we go $300 further into debt.

Dad comes through the door. I greet him with you in my arms. I have managed to pull together some dinner even though you were fussy all day. He steps over the laundry and toys on the floor and hugs me. He is tired but his eyes are always so kind. I pass you to him and stir the soup I have simmering on the stove.

I can feel the tightness in my throat again. It comes when I think too much about how things have turned out. We were not supposed to be this poor. We were supposed to graduate and get jobs. We were not supposed to struggle this hard. Didn't we get educated so we could be better off? We are actually worse off than if we hadn't gone to university, because we have our school debt. We also could have had four years of work and experience under our belts.

I fill our bowls and we sit at the tiny round table in our kitchen. Dad looks at the pile of mail. It is all unopened. Some of the envelope windows show pink letters inside. He sighs. I know how hard he is working and I cannot help right now. You are too small. It would be futile for me to work for minimum wage and pay for daycare. My wages would simply go to our caregiver.

"So, what do you want to do?" I ask.

"I think we will have to ask your parents for help," he says.

"I know," I manage to mumble and feel the defeat rise up in my chest.

We move in with Grandma and Grandpa the next weekend and give our landlord notice. The welfare cheques stop, but the bills keep coming. At least there is a roof over our heads and food on the table.

A few months later, Dad finds a government program that helps young people find employment. The government pays a large portion of the young person's wage which gives the employer incentive to provide them with work and much-needed employment experience. It is a great fit for his carpentry skills. It's a window- and door-installation business. Dad is excited to be working with his hands and in a stable place, at least while the grant lasts.

Seven months later, we are moving out of Grandma and Grandpa's house into our own apartment in the city. I hate paying rent, but at least it's our own place. Dad is still at the window and door company, and we have saved up enough for first and last month's rent. You are enamoured with the stairs that go down to this basement apartment and I am thrilled with the shorter commute Dad has to and from work.

"Hey Kirsten, I've met someone I think can help us get our own house," Dad says a few months after we moved to our own apartment.

"Really? But we don't have a down payment," I say skeptically.

"I know. This guy says there is something called a long-form mortgage. We would make monthly rent payments but after a year those payments would represent our down payment, and it would be sufficient to demonstrate to a bank that we could carry the mortgage," he explains.

I can't believe it. It has only been six months in our apartment and now we might have a house. I try not to get too excited, but I would feel so much better not paying rent and starting to really create a life for you.

"I have other news too," Dad says. "The owners of the window and door business want out. They are tired of the creditors calling. The business is at least $50,000 in debt, maybe more, and they are talking about letting me take it over."

I don't see this as great news like Dad does. The debt is too much. I cannot think about those sorts of numbers. We are having a hard enough time paying our monthly student loans for a couple hundred a month, how will we manage thousands? I can feel the panic rising in me, but when I look over at Dad he looks so confident. He is ready to do anything to change our situation.

"We can move the business phone number to our new house and run the business from there," he adds.

I try to get on board. I am so used to the phone ringing with creditors wanting money, what's the difference with having another phone line in the house doing the same?

"Okay. Let's try this. What have we got to lose anyway?" I say. I start thinking of more ways I can try to save money and how I can help with the business. I will bake bread from scratch. We will eat simple homemade foods. I will do the bookkeeping and answer the phones with you here at my feet. I might even throw on a tool belt to help now and then.

Dad sees me coming around. He gets up from his seat and wraps his arms around me. He whispers in my ear, "We might have nothing, but I think we have everything." He's right. We are together. We are working hard and trying to make things right as a team. We are clawing our way out of the bottom. This is abundance, right here, even if we have less than nothing.

Dad sits again, smiles, and eats his soup.

You Are More Than Your Titles

Cody, age 13. Me, age 36.

Dad and I navigate through the early morning traffic and pull up at the address of this week's kitchen installation. It's a home in one of the nicer neighbourhoods of Calgary. Dad backs the van onto the exposed aggregate concrete driveway and I look over at the impeccably manicured lawns and flower beds. I jump out of the van in my work jeans and T-shirt with my hair pulled back into a ponytail. This is a dirty job, so there is no need for fancy clothes, and it is safer for me to have my hair out of my face while I work. I still struggle with looking a little frumpy on the job though.

Dad rings the doorbell and a man in golf attire opens it. He has that silver-fox look and greets Dad with a warm handshake. The man glances over at me and says to Dad, "I see you brought along some help today. Isn't that sweet!" Blood runs up the back of my neck and into my cheeks. Dad simply nods and smiles and makes his way across the threshold. It takes everything in me not to turn around and head back to the van. How dare he think this is "sweet!" I am not here to bake cookies and sweep up after "my man." I am here to work as an equal partner and I can wield a drill with the best of them.

After a quick tour of the space, Dad and I fall into our usual rhythm. We begin hauling in the cabinets, floor coverings, and tools. Dad and I don't need to talk to each other while we work, as we have been doing this together long enough that we know what needs to be done. The homeowner is watching as I work and I can see him stealing a glance now and then to double check what I am doing. I know his type well, so I engage him in conversation.

"So, what do you do? Are you retired?" I ask.

"Yes and no," he says. "I still do some consulting for an oil company."

"You could say I am retired too," I joke. "I finished my corporate job and decided to work with my husband as my retirement."

He laughs. I only partially feel better after letting him know I've done other things. I move on with making his kitchen beautiful, but inside I know it was petty to prove to him I had more to offer than my carpentry skills. I still feel the need to be more than a kitchen installer's helper. I am clinging to my last real title. I want to feel important again, but my title was stripped away when I left that job. It is hard to go from a job of prestige to a blue-collar worker. I am embarrassed. I feel like no one will take me seriously and that I am a failure. It hurts because it's partially true; I have failed at figuring out what I want to do next. I am working with Dad because I am afraid to try something on my own, and without my title, I just don't know if I can find fulfilment.

I have tried to find fulfilment in every possible way in life. I was near the top of my class for fulfilment, if there is such a thing. I got the education I thought would fulfil me. I got married to fulfil me. I had a baby to fulfil me. I worked hard in my job to gain skills and get promoted to fulfil me. I acquired all the titles I thought were important: scholar, wife, mother, and manager. And guess what? None of them have led to the fulfilment I thought would come from them. The truth is, I am more than my titles and I have to learn that I do not need them to be happy or to be engaged in life.

I still have the same brain, the same skills, and the same talents. I just happen to be sanding and staining kitchens. I need to stop judging myself and see that I am just as valuable no matter what my station is.

I can still have incredible impact on those around me. I can still contribute to making the world a better place. I can still love and give and encourage. I can view myself in a broader sense. Am I using my skills and abilities, my connections, and my time and resources to the best of my abilities? That definition of success is so much more than a title.

So far you have rejected the titles I sought at your age. You are not concerned about being a scholar, top of your class, or super popular. You are satisfied to define yourself outside these labels. You are so much more able to create perspective around that than I am. You tell me not to buy you any clothes with brands visible on them, because you "aren't a poser." You don't need a shirt brand to fit in. I just hope that you keep this strong definition of who you are and let the titles come and go without worry.

Freedom Is Responsibility

Cody, age 16. Me, age 39.

I really want to go away on our camping vacation, without you. You are just too big to fit in your makeshift bunk in the back of the van, and I don't want you rolling your eyes at everything we want to do. You also have a summer job this year and could use the shifts. You tell me you can stay home by yourself, but I am so worried about what will go on. I am not naive. I know you will have some friends over. I know there might be girls. I know there might be drinking too.

"I can handle it," you say, trying to persuade me to let you stay alone.

"He can handle it," Dad adds to the convincing.

"But what if he has a party?" I argue.

"He probably will have a party," Dad says and glances over at you.

"Maybe a few friends, but I will make sure it doesn't get out of hand, promise," you offer.

"But what if it goes viral and tons of people end up at the party?" I ask, knowing how things can get out of hand with social media in bigger cities.

"I'll get a baseball bat and clear the house," you say, puffing up your chest and slamming your fist into your hand.

"Yeah, ummm, no. Wrong answer," Dad interjects. "You will go into the bathroom, pull out your cell phone, and call the cops on your own party. No one needs to know you called and you will stay safe."

We let you stay home alone and we go on vacation without you. Of course we gave a heads up to the neighbours first.

As we are pulling into the driveway when we return, I am already scanning for evidence. Are there broken windows? Are there bottles or cans in the grass? I open the front door and notice that someone has made an attempt to clean. The wipe marks on the floor are pretty visible. It's not as clean as I would like it, but the effort is nice nonetheless. I check the ceiling and walls for holes. Nothing. I check the bathroom for puke splatters. So far so good. And then from across the room I can see it under the couch. A single bottle cap. Aha!

"How was the party?" I ask.

"I just had a few people over," you answer.

"Was there a lot of drinking?" I inquire.

"Well, a bit," you mumble.

"Did you let anyone drive after drinking?" I probe, raising my eyebrow.

"No. Everyone stayed over and left in the morning," you say, like any other answer would be absurd.

"And they helped clean up?" I ask playfully.

"No. I had to do it all on my own. I won't do that again," you grumble.

I smile to myself at the lesson learned for us both.

Letting you stay home alone was freedom for us and for you, but something else was happening too. In the midst of that freedom you were forced to step into responsibility again, just like you have had to throughout your upbringing.

You have Dad to thank for your childhood freedoms. I would have fallen prey to my fears of what could happen. In my fear, I might

158

not have let you go enough to let you bruise your knees, have to clean up your messes, or even fail. Dad helped; he made me loosen my grip.

I didn't want you attached to a TV screen with the umbilical cord of your gaming controller, but I also didn't want you to out alone in the big bad world.

I had to learn that freedom is more than just being able to play outside alone. It is about extending your boundaries as you grow. You forced us to figure this out. I can remember you looking directly at me as a toddler while you touched something I had just told you not to. In your own toddler way, you were telling me that you were testing your boundaries but also expressing that you wanted more freedom. You had a will. You had autonomy. It was counterintuitive; your behaviour made me want to restrict you further, but instead I learned to raise your responsibility. You were pushing at the edges to grow into something new.

Freedom and responsibility are the same thing. I didn't make this connection when you were young, but I have finally figured it out. When we are extending freedom to you, we are also giving you the responsibility that goes with it. "Go play in the park with your friends" comes with remembering what time to come home, watching out for dangers, and the social responsibility of playing fairly with peers. "Yes, you can borrow the car" comes with driving safely, filling it up with gas with your own money, and owning up to a fender bender (luckily there has only been one). "Yes, you can stay home alone" comes with cleaning up and staying safe.

If I hover over you because of my fears, I will stifle your growth. I will prevent you from developing confidence, and I will undermine your respect by demonstrating that I don't trust you.

Giving you room to grow is more work than helicopter parenting. It requires thought and structure, and coaching and mentoring. It also means learning to separate myself from your behaviour (good or bad). It is messy and hard. Extending you freedom means I have to loosen my grip. Extending you freedom means I have to trust you. But extending you freedom will build your responsibility, and what type of parent would I be if I didn't give you that?

SECTION 7: UNTIL NEXT TIME (CONCLUSION)

In the End, There Is Only You

Cody, age 6. Me, age 29.

Feverish, impromptu huddles of my staff are cropping up around the store. I overhear someone saying, "There are planes driving into the Twin Towers and the Pentagon." I watch as more and more staff leave the store and head out into the mall to see for themselves. I follow along to the Sony store. There in grotesque repetition across screen after screen. I see the planes and smoke and crumbling buildings. I see the usual stoic news anchors looking shaken. I stand there with other people frozen in disbelief and I try to make sense of what is happening along with the rest of the world.

Numbly I return to the store. I have to. We are only nine days from our grand opening, and as one of five managers I have too much to do. My cosmetic fixtures aren't wired for light and power yet. Parts of the store don't have any walls. We still don't have phone lines or network cables. Most of the merchandise is still to arrive. I am putting on my calm but purposeful face to keep everyone working toward the deadline, but I still wonder if things will come together in time. This tragedy is happening somewhere else, and I try to push it from my mind to focus on what I need to get done.

I look down at my clipboard to remember what I was working on before I went out into the mall. When I look up I see one of my staff approaching. I can see other people look up from various tasks and watch her walk toward me. She is the messenger. She stops in front of me and my stomach clenches as I look into her unguarded eyes. Her weight is shifting from foot to foot as she tries to get some words out. "There is some talk about the possibility of our men needing to be deployed. I want to be here helping out with the store but I just don't know if my husband will need to leave at a moment's notice, and I want to be able to say goodbye." She tries to mask the hitch in her voice with a cough but I feel the emotion behind her words as the hairs on my arms stand up.

She is not the only serviceman's wife and I know she is speaking on behalf of all of them. I could send her home but then the rest of the wives would go home too, and we need them. Instead the managers call an emergency meeting with the facilities team and we work to get some emergency phone lines in place. That is enough security for the staff to be able to work and still feel connected to their families at home.

I am drained from the effort of the past few hours and days. I pass my clipboard on to my team lead and head home. It's only a five-minute drive to our house from the store, but I don't remember the drive. It is early afternoon and nobody is home yet. You are still in school and Dad is working. I unlock the front door and drop my keys on the kitchen table. The house is quiet and the air stale from being closed up for the day. I fall heavily into a chair in the living room and stare blankly out the window.

I am not seeing outside. I am seeing the planes, the smoke, and the fear in my staff's eyes. A future of war rises before me. I wonder if Dad will be called to serve too. I know we don't have conscription in Canada, but my world has been rocked and I am not quite sure of anything anymore. You come into my mind. You are only six. You are all rambunctious skinned knees, curious dirty hands, and innocent possibility. What kind of a world are you going to have to live in? I think of packing us up and trying to hide somewhere but I don't know where we could go. Will you even have a chance to grow up?

The world outside the window comes into focus. I look at the sky and its familiar shade of blue. The trees in our yard are swaying in the afternoon breeze and I can hear the birds singing. They haven't stopped to ponder the plight of the humans. They are still busy getting on with their lives, digging for worms, singing for their territories, and flitting from tree to tree. The trees and sky don't seem to care either. There is such serenity in nature, but inside my head there is chaos and uncertainty. What if I will have to raise you alone? What if I will have to endure loss after loss of people I love during a war? What if I can't provide a safe world for you to grow up in? What then?

I continue to stare out the window. The sun is still shining and the birds are still singing. I have been holding my breath, but now I breathe out a long sigh. A thought crosses my mind: "I have everything I need right now, right here, exactly as things are." I have me. I imagine laying on my back looking up at the blue sky with the treetops gently swaying in the breeze. What would it be like if this were my final view while dying? I am surprised that I feel peaceful, not terrified. Though I am all alone here in death, I am not really alone. I have everything right here with me that I have always had, because I have me.

It will not matter if someone is here beside me in these final moments. It will not matter if someone is holding my hand. In these last moments on earth, I am only reflecting deeply with myself. The tough questions come to me: "What was it like to live?" and "Did you have a good life?" I feel the anger swell up as I think about how much of my life I have lived trying to meet other people's expectations. But that is quickly replaced with another question: "Did I live up to my expectations?" Did I do everything I wanted to? Was I true to myself? Did I learn and love and listen to my heart? Right here, in the end, I only have one person to answer to. Right here, in the end, there is only me.

I am face to face with my mortality, and though I have loved others and was loved by others, the only question that remains is "Did I love me?" At every twist and turn in my life, this question has been there. I am my only constant companion through every experience, and it is such a long journey to not enjoy my own company. I am still striving at being good at loving and being alone with myself. I am still working on weighing my expectations above all others.

I hear the front door open and you walk in with your backpack. You kick off your shoes one at a time and they land wherever your foot flings them. They are permanently tied, loose-fitting shoes, just the way you like them.

I want to release you from my expectations.

You smile a partially toothless smile when you see that it is me not Dad who is home. I am rarely home after school for you.

I want you to hasten your ability to love yourself.

You open the fridge and leave a sweaty boy-dirty handprint on the handle and ask if you can have a juice box.

I wish you a long journey with you, a strong and powerful you, by your side.

ACKNOWLEDGEMENTS

To my husband, Schaene: without you there would have been no stories to tell and no time to sit and write to tell them. Thank you for your unending support and love.

To my son, Cody: thank you for teaching me as much or more than I taught you. Thank you for your permission to write this book and, as you said, "do my thing."

Before there was even a full book, there were two other people who encouraged me daily to get my words on a page. Thank you to the rest of the Book or Bust group, Shandra Carlson and Stephanie Pollock.

To my early readers, Brenda Ball, Jean-Michel Gires, Dana Goldstein, Stephanie Pollock, and Melanie Simpson: I appreciate for your candid feedback and buoying my spirits in the ugly first-draft stage. It is invaluable to have champions.

To my editors, Chantel Hamilton and Jaclyn Arndt: you have my gratitude for holding my hand through my first book. You made the process easy and dramatically improved the book from its first version.

And finally, a heartfelt thanks to my friends and family who lived alongside me for the first half of my life. Here's to an amazing second half!

I am blessed by all your support.

THANK YOU

I wish to extend a big thank you to my book support members. They were instrumental in providing feedback, getting the word out, and helping to shape this book.

I am grateful to each of you:

Brenda Ball, Carla Ciepliski, Chris Enstrom, Jean-Michel Gires, Dana Goldstein, Suzanne Gunn, Chantel Hamilton, Heidi Johnson, Lisa Ingram, Jill Langer, Bob Mcinnis, Isidra Mencos, Kelly Morrison, Stephanie Pollock, Calvin Simpson, Melanie Simpson, Jennifer Smyth, Cheryl Strachan, John Weirick, and Dolores Wreggitt.

ABOUT THE AUTHOR

"Average lives can be extraordinary." —*Kirsten Wreggitt*

Kirsten Wreggitt grew up in a small town in the middle of the Great Lakes region. Her big heart and curious mind have taken her on a few journeys through a couple of relocations, careers, and roles. Each opportunity has shaped her view of the world and sparked another journey into more curiosity and reflection. She currently lives, writes, and works in Calgary, Alberta.

You can read more of her writing at www.kirstenwreggitt.com and while you are there subscribe to her weekly newsletter and receive a FREE copy of her manifesto, "Average is Extraordinary: How Your Life is Anything But Mediocre."

Made in the USA
Columbia, SC
26 December 2017